JIT Implementation Manual

The Complete Guide to
Just-in-Time Manufacturing

Second Edition

JIT Implementation Manual

The Complete Guide to
Just-in-Time Manufacturing

Second Edition

Volume 1
The Just-in-Time Production System

HIROYUKI HIRANO

CRC Press
Taylor & Francis Group
Boca Raton   London   New York

CRC Press is an imprint of the
Taylor & Francis Group, an **informa** business

A PRODUCTIVITY PRESS BOOK

CRC Press
Taylor & Francis Group
6000 Broken Sound Parkway NW, Suite 300
Boca Raton, FL 33487-2742

Contents

Publisher's Message ix

Foreword to the Original English Edition xi

Introduction to the Original English Edition xiii

Volume 1

1   Production Management and JIT Production Management 1

Approach to Production Management 3

Overview of the JIT Production System 7

Introduction of the JIT Production System 12

2   Destroying Factory Myths: A Revolutionary Approach 35

Relations among Sales Price, Cost, and Profit 35

Ten Arguments against the JIT Production Revolution 40

Approach to Production as a Whole 44

Index I-1

About the Author I-31

Volume 2

3   "Wastology": The Total Elimination of Waste 145

Why Does Waste Occur? 146

Types of Waste 151

How to Discover Waste 179

How to Remove Waste 198

Secrets for Not Creating Waste 226

4   The "5S" Approach 237

What Are the 5S's? 237

Red Tags and Signboards: Proper Arrangement and
Orderliness Made Visible 265

The Red Tag Strategy for Visual Control 268

The Signboard Strategy: Visual Orderliness 293

Orderliness Applied to Jigs and Tools................................307

Volume 3

5   Flow Production **321**

Why Inventory Is Bad...321

What Is Flow Production? 328

Flow Production within and between Factories.....................332

6   Multi-Process Operations **387**

Multi-Process Operations: A Wellspring for Humanity on the Job.....387

The Difference between Horizontal Multi-Unit Operations and

Vertical Multi-Process Operations 388

Questions and Key Points about Multi-Process Operations.............393

Precautions and Procedures for Developing Multi-Process

Operations 404

7   Labor Cost Reduction **415**

What Is Labor Cost Reduction? 415

Labor Cost Reduction Steps 419

Points for Achieving Labor Cost Reduction 422

Visible Labor Cost Reduction 432

8   *Kanban* **435**

Differences between the *Kanban* System and Conventional Systems...435

Functions and Rules of *Kanban* 440

How to Determine the Variety and Quantity of *Kanban*..............442

Administration of *Kanban* 447

9   Visual Control..**453**

What Is Visual Control?..453

Case Study: Visual Orderliness (*Seiton*)...............................459

Standing Signboards 462

Andon: Illuminating Problems in the Factory 464

Production Management Boards: At-a-Glance Supervision.............470

Relationship between Visual Control and *Kaizen* 471

Volume 4

10 Leveling 475

What Is Level Production? 475

Various Ways to Create Production Schedules 477

Differences between Shish-Kabob Production and Level Production 482

Leveling Techniques 485

Realizing Production Leveling 492

11 Changeover 497

Why Is Changeover Improvement (*Kaizen*) Necessary? 497

What Is Changeover? 498

Procedure for Changeover Improvement 500

Seven Rules for Improving Changeover 532

12 Quality Assurance 541

Quality Assurance: The Starting Point in Building Products 541

Structures that Help Identify Defects 546

Overall Plan for Achieving Zero Defects 561

The *Poka-Yoke* System 566

Poka-Yoke Case Studies for Various Defects 586

How to Use *Poka-Yoke* and Zero Defects Checklists 616

Volume 5

13 Standard Operations 623

Overview of Standard Operations 623

How to Establish Standard Operations 628

How to Make Combination Charts and Standard Operations Charts....630

Standard Operations and Operation Improvements.........................638

How to Preserve Standard Operations 650

14 *Jidoka:* Human Automation 655

Steps toward *Jidoka* 655

The Difference between Automation and *Jidoka* 657

The Three Functions of *Jidoka* 658

Separating Workers: Separating Human Work from Machine Work 660

Ways to Prevent Defects 672

Extension of *Jidoka* to the Assembly Line......................................676

15 Maintenance and Safety **683**

Existing Maintenance Conditions on the Factory Floor 683

What Is Maintenance? 684

CCO: Three Lessons in Maintenance 689

Preventing Breakdowns 683

Why Do Injuries Occur? 685

What Is Safety? 688

Strategies for Zero Injuries and Zero Accidents 689

Volume 6

16 JIT Forms 711

Overall Management 715

Waste-Related Forms 730

5S-Related Forms 747

Engineering-Related Forms 777

JIT Introduction-Related Forms 834

Publisher's Message

Hiroyuki Hirano's *JIT Implementation Manual* was first published in Japan in 1989, and Productivity Press published the English translation the following year. In his Foreword to the original English edition, Norman Bodek refers to the book as a "masterpiece," and it has certainly stood the test of time and proven itself during the past twenty years.

This was the first work of its kind to provide, in such great detail, a structured approach to the implementation of what was commonly referred to as "just-in-time" manufacturing, and to cover so many of the concepts that are core to what we now call "lean manufacturing"—identification and elimination of waste, visual management, the 5S's, flow production, *kanban*, cellular manufacturing, leveling, quick changeover, poka-yoke, standard work, *jidoka*, and so much more.

Mr. Hirano refers to 1989 and 1990 as pivotal years in the transformation of Japan's industrial structure, and what better time than the economic transition we are experiencing in 2009 to re-release this classic work.

The first edition, now out of print, comprised two binders in a slipcase. In this new edition, prompted by many requests from long-time users of the original volumes, we provide the same information in a more accessible format. These six paperback volumes contain all the original, unedited material from the original edition, divided into logical sections that follow the steps Mr. Hirano details for establishing a JIT production system (see Figure 1.6 in Volume 1, Chapter 1):

Volume 1 Step 1 – Awareness Revolution
Volume 2 Step 2 – The 5S's for factory improvement
Volume 3 Step 3 – Flow manufacturing
Volume 4 Step 4 - Leveling
Volume 5 Step 5 - Standardized operations
Volume 6 The JIT forms

In addition, we have included a CD containing PDFs of all the forms in Volume 6 so readers can easily print the individual forms in multiples, or use them as models for creating custom forms. Of course, the point of the forms is to promote engagement of all team members and focus on improvement activities – not to complete them in isolation and house them in a cabinet or on a hard drive! We have also added a detailed index for the entire set of six volumes. For your convenience, the complete index is included in each volume.

We hope that students, those interested in the roots of lean, and those many practitioners who have requested that this information be brought back into print will benefit from this new release.

Maura May
Publisher

Foreword to the Original English Edition

A year ago Productivity Press published what we considered to be the best introduction for all employees to Just-In-Time (JIT)—a picture book entitled *JIT Factory Revolution: A Pictorial Guide to Factory Design of the Future* by Hiroyuki Hirano, a top international consultant. I am now proud to offer you its counterpart—the most comprehensive and detailed manual in the world today for setting up a complete JIT program. *JIT Implementation Manual: The Complete Guide to Just-In-Time Manufacturing* is also written by Mr. Hirano, who is really making his genius accessible for the first time. At last we have a place to go to get answers to virtually every JIT problem.

One evening in January 1990, I had dinner with Mr. Hirano and his wife at a very lovely French restaurant in Tokyo. I told him how pleased I was with his work and then asked him to explain exactly what he does in his consulting practice. He started off by showing how he uses one of his forms. He gathers his client's conversion team and reviews the homework left from his last visit. Each member explains the improvements made within the plant. Afterwards, carrying a pad of these forms, each person follows him around the plant, where up to 100 problems are identified, indicated by type (for instance, the 5S's, one-piece flow, visual management, multi-process workers, *jidoka*, leveling, work standardization), and recorded on the forms. The forms are then posted on bulletin boards and become homework for his next visit. This is the simple, but very powerful, Hirano method of focusing on improvement activities. And his manual is filled with similar practical examples from his own highly successful consulting practice.

In an extremely well-written and articulate presentation, this manual provides a clear structure that enables readers to easily ferret out vital information. The material is addressed in three sections: JIT concepts, JIT techniques, and actual tools for putting JIT into practice. Based on his vast experience in factories throughout Asia and the West, Mr. Hirano explains in detail over 200 illustrations, charts, checklists, diagrams, and sample JIT management forms that he uses to implement "JIT Awareness Revolutions" wherever he goes. This massive handbook contains answers to virtually every problem a JIT professional will face, as well as multiple options for every stage of JIT implementation.

If I sound effusive, please understand that I have been searching for such a resource to offer Productivity Press readers for years. In fact, throughout the 1980s, Productivity's industrial study missions to Japan revolved around my personal quest to find the best source materials for implementing JIT. And while we have come across numerous consultants and engineers and translated many superb books and materials, I have waited a long time for a handbook of the caliber of Hiroyuki Hirano's *JIT Implementation Manual*.

This is Productivity Press's most ambitious publishing project to date. Known as the "JIT Bible" in Japan, Mr. Hirano's *JIT Implementation Manual* is encyclopedic in scope and provides unparalleled information on every aspect of JIT, from its philosophical underpinnings to the myriad systems, techniques, and tools for virtually every factory setting.

To produce this massive project as quickly as possible, many fine people—both Productivity staff and freelance professionals—were employed. In particular, I wish to acknowledge the efforts of: Bruce Talbot for his splendid translation and writing; Cheryl Berling Rosen for her editorial and content supervision; David Lennon and Esme McTighe for their production management; Sally Schwager for her bilingual handling of the numerous queries between Mr. Hirano and the Productivity staff; Tim Sandler for his copyediting; and Micki Amick of Amick Communications for the manual's design, page makeup, art production, and project management.

Our mission at Productivity is to publish and distribute the best materials on productivity, quality improvement, and employee involvement for business and industry, academia, and the general public. Many of our products, like the Hirano manual, are direct source materials from Japan that we have translated into English for the first time. It is with great anticipation that I present this work to our readers. I thank Mr. Hiroyuki Hirano for granting us the opportunity to produce this masterpiece in English.

Norman Bodek
Publisher

Introduction to the Original English Edition

In the future, I think we shall look back upon 1989 and 1990 as pivotal years in the transformation of Japan's industrial structure.

During these years, abiding yen appreciation and trade friction will continue to devalue the advantages of Japanese domestic production. As a result, we will see more and more Japanese automakers, electronics firms, and other manufacturers shifting their production overseas.

Japan's large "parent" companies are heading overseas in droves, leaving behind their "child" subcontractors. It would be nice if the parent companies could take their children with them, but the children generally lack the money, staff, technology, and marketing power to make the move. So the children are left behind to fend for themselves. They are entering a bitter battle for survival, in which many must enter into new industrial fields to pull through.

The high yen and the search for lower costs has also boosted the flow of Japan's imports from the Asian NIES (Newly Industrialized Economic Societies) and the ASEAN countries. These parts and products are generally characterized by large volumes, unhurried schedules for production and delivery, and relatively lenient quality standards. By the same token, the goods that are still produced in Japan tend to have the opposite characteristics—small volumes, tight production and delivery schedules, top-notch quality, and marketable prices.

Japan's ongoing trend toward market diversification has further fueled the demands for wide-variety, small-lot production with speedy delivery. Let it be understood at the outset that JIT production is neither one automaker's production system nor is it the subcontractor's curse. Instead, JIT consists of *ideas and techniques for the complete elimination of waste*.

In a sense, JIT production is a new field of industrial engineering (IE), one that thoroughly eliminates the waste that runs rampant in most factories while helping to build products that serve client needs. JIT production is also the kind of market-oriented or "market-in" production system that is increasingly needed in today's fast-changing global marketplace.

This book is a compendium of the experiences and knowledge I have gained during many years of enthusiastic work in battling waste in factories and promoting the development of JIT production. As such, this is a manual for professional consultants. It enables them to tell the plain truth and to overcome vexing problems.

This book is not for sale to the general public. I would not want it to be sold that way. It is a book for manufacturing companies that are fighting desperately for survival and that will go to any length to improve their factories and overcome the obstacles to success. One could even call this book a "bible" for corporate survival.

Accordingly, this book is intended for only three types of readers: leading strategists for corporate survival, including top management; in-house JIT leaders; and professional JIT consultants.

Chapters 1 and 2 describe the JIT production approach and its underlying concepts. As you will see, the JIT approach casts off old concepts and introduces a revolutionary way of thinking.

Chapter 3 looks into the nature of waste and tells how we can scientifically identify waste and take comprehensive steps to remove it.

Chapter 4 takes up the 5S's, which make up the foundation for making improvements in factories. This chapter will pay special attention to red-tagging and *kanban* techniques as devices for visual control and regulation of the factory.

Chapters 5 to 15 present explanations, backed by many case studies, of JIT techniques centered on flow manufacturing.

Finally, Chapter 16 includes a large selection of vouchers, lists, and other JIT-related forms, many of which can be photocopied and used as is. These forms can serve as effective tools in paving the way for JIT production.

This manual broadly falls into three parts. The first part presents JIT concepts, the middle part JIT techniques, and the last part tools for putting JIT into practice.

I will conclude by asking those of you who use this manual to avoid taking a piecemeal approach, such as adopting only the *kanban* or *andon* systems or aiming at only a limited range of improvements. The overall flow is the most important aspect of production, and the key ingredient for creating a good overall flow is comprehensive improvement—in other words, factory-based innovation. If readers understand this book and find it useful as a "bible" for building better products, I will gain the satisfaction of knowing that the five years of effort and expense invested in this project since its planning stage were not just another form of waste.

Hiroyuki Hirano
February 1989

Chapter 1

Production Management and JIT Production Management

In today's world, manufacturing industries can no longer afford to remain complacent in the belief that their chief concern is to turn out products.

Things were quite different during the early postwar years, which marked the birth of Japan's modern industry. Basic materials—even for such things as shoes and clothing—were extremely scarce. Anyone who could scrape together enough materials to make a product could sell it. The successful manufacturers were simply those who had access to materials.

How things have changed. Today, clothing and shoe stores are everywhere, their shelves jam-packed with merchandise. Long gone are the days when Japan's manufacturers could sell whatever they could make. Now there are literally thousands of clothing and footwear manufacturers in Japan, and there must be hundreds of thousands worldwide.

The simple, hard-nosed approach that says, "Manufacturing is the business of making things," has grown dangerously out of date. To become a winner in today's survival game, manufacturers must make big changes in their way of thinking. For today, the key to successful factory management is the realization that *manufacturing is a service industry*.

Until quite recently, the common orientation among manufacturers was, "Make good products cheaply and quickly." This approach became known as the QCD (Quality, Cost, and Delivery) approach. The QCD approach was a reliable road to success for many years, but today it takes more than these three elements to ensure a factory's survival. Three additional conditions are now evident:

1. *Diversification*

   The growing diversity of customer needs is accelerating the trend toward greater varieties of products on the market.

2. *Smaller lots*

   The total market pie is not growing much larger, but the variety of products are. So, naturally, these products have to be made in smaller lots.

3. *Shorter delivery schedules*

   As the product diversification trend continues, companies will go broke if they stick to their old habit of keeping full-line inventories. But what are the alternatives? It is not easy to predict which product types will sell best and in what volumes. So companies instead try to replace warehoused products as soon as they are sold, or they switch over to special-order production with short delivery schedules.

When taken together, these three conditions call for "wide-variety, small-lot production with speedy delivery."

This means adding new elements to the old tripartite QCD formula to accommodate product diversification. Today, we need to add a "P" for product diversification and an "S" for safety. The result is the PQCDS approach, a service-oriented approach attuned to current needs (Figure 1.1).

To put it another way, PQCDS is a service that manufacturers provide by making desired products (P) of high quality (Q) at low cost (C) with speedy delivery (D) and assured safety (S) from start to finish.

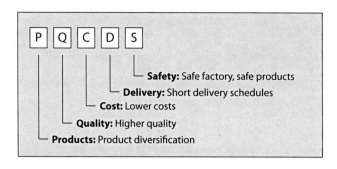

Figure 1.1　The PQCDS Approach.

Here we have an important transition from being a product maker to becoming a service provider. Today, manufacturers must think of themselves as service-industry companies.

Approach to Production Management

Many a factory manager has asked me: "We're using a computer-based production management system now, but for some reason we have not been able to reduce our warehouse inventories or shorter lead-times. What should we do?" (See Chapter 2 for an additional discussion of the JIT approach to warehousing and lead-times.)

For some reason, even top managers at factories seem to think of the computer as some kind of magic wand. They somehow reckon that once a computer-based system is installed, the factory will run like a finely crafted timepiece.

I always answer this question the same way: "First you have to change the president's mind!" That's all there is to it.

Let us begin by looking at the issue of lead-time. Generally, we define a product's lead-time as the period that begins when the sales department issues the production plan and ends when the planned products is shipped.

Figure 1.2 takes a somewhat closer look at the various elements within the lead-time.

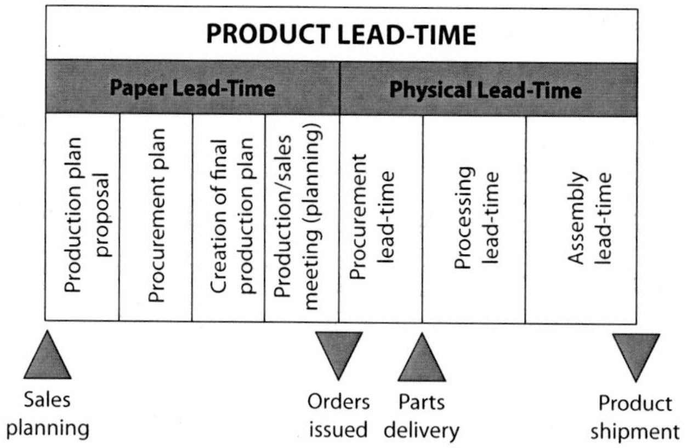

Figure 1.2 Product Lead-Time.

Obviously, a factory cannot go immediately from receiving a sales plan to building products. The factory managers must first size up the production capacity situation and then begin working out a production plan proposal. Next, the production and sales departments need to meet, tailor the proposal to their specific needs, and jointly approve it.

Once the proposal has been revised and approved, it needs to be rewritten as the official production schedule, which includes delivery schedules for the assembly components and other parts and materials required by the schedule. The official production schedule also includes instructions for goods procurement and subcontractor orders.

During all of these stages, the clock is ticking but no products are being manufactured. All that has happened so far is planning, which is to say paper-shuffling and number-crunching. Still, we are obliged to include these time-consuming planning processes as part of the overall lead-time. So, before actually making anything, there is lots of paperwork, which led me to call this part of the overall lead-time the *paper lead-time.*

By contrast, three-dimensional materials really start moving once the production orders are issued and the products are shipped. First, the procurement people and the subcontractors get moving when the order book is out. Soon, deliveries of procured and subcontracted products start arriving. Then the factory gets into gear, using equipment such as cutters, presses, and lathes to process and assemble parts. Once the parts are finished, they can be assembled into finished products.

Naturally, various kinds of information have been exchanged throughout these stages, and the flow of production has been firmly centered on the work in process. The key issues invariably are: how to process the materials, which manual operations to use, and how to move things around. That is why I call this latter part of the overall lead-time the *physical lead-time.*

If we introduce computerization to shorten lead-times, what distinct effects might such a move have on the paper lead-time and the physical lead-time? Let's first look at the possible effects on the paper lead-time.

It is not difficult to imagine the kind of time and energy it takes when people get together with their calculators to work out the numbers for an efficient production schedule. To make the production schedule work efficiently, these planners have to calculate the correct amounts of various parts and materials, as well as the proper timing for their delivery.

A computer can be very helpful in facilitating and speeding these paper lead-time tasks. But just how helpful can it be in shortening the physical lead-time?

For instance, if a factory manager tells a subcontractor, "We just got a computer to help run our factory," is the subcontractor supposed to think he needs to start delivering his products to the factory in half the time? Or is the subcontractor foolish enough to think that installing a computer in his own factory will enable half-day change-over procedures to be drastically reduced?

To shorten the physical lead-time portion of the overall lead-time, we need something other than computers. Usually, we need factory-based improvements. We call the kind of factory-based improvements that result from adopting Just-In-Time "JIT improvements."

Thus, the fact is that computers mainly help shorten the paper lead-time by improving clerical processes. It is only by

DEFINITION OF PRODUCTION MANAGEMENT

Production management means building and commanding:

a management system (organization framework, procedures, information, management techniques, and other information-based organizing factors) and

a physical system (plant equipment, equipment layout, production methods, conveyance methods, and other equipment-based organizing factors)

while making effective use of the three M's (manpower, materials, and machines) to economically manufacture products of a certain value and quality, in certain volume and within a certain period of time.

Figure 1.3   Production Management Defined.

getting involved in making factory-based improvements that we can effectively shorten the physical lead-time. Our tactics should differ depending on which kind of lead-time we are trying to shorten.

In the factory, we are faced with a wide range of problems and issues. It is the job of production management to sort out and correct these problems according to market needs.

We should ask ourselves the simple question, "What is production management?" To answer that question, we need to return to the basics. Consider the definition of production management on Figure 1.3.

Factories should be thought of as living entities or organic systems. Within the factory's overall system are information-based factors that are hard to see, and equipment-based factors involving the flow of goods that are easier to see.

We refer to the overall system's information-based factors as the management system and its equipment-based factors as the physical system. The management system includes such things as the factory's organization, its hierarchy or organizing framework, its clerical procedures, and other information-related aspects that readily lend themselves to improvement through computerization. By contrast, the physical system includes the plant equipment and its layout within the factory, production methods, and other equipment-related aspects.

Today, factories are grappling with a common problem: how to combine the management system and physical system so that they function together in a level manner, like the two axles of an automobile, while serving current needs for wide product variety, high quality, low costs, and speedy delivery.

It is all well and good to bring computerization into the information-related aspects, but that will not do much good if the company's organization remains in the mass-production mode of decades past and the manufacturing orientation still emphasizes large lots. Conversely, companies will find themselves lagging behind the times if they concentrate solely on factory-floor improvements and ignore the advantages of computerized information management.

From a comprehensive standpoint, we can make a distinction between "JIT production management" as a program for developing production management attuned to market needs and "JIT improvements" as a program for improving efforts centered on a factory's physical system.

As the two axles of the "factory automobile," the management system and the physical system must be kept in pace with each other, with neither being pushed ahead or held back relative to the other. Otherwise, the automobile will not get to its destination of corporate success.

Overview of the JIT Production System

The JIT production system is a market-oriented production system that rests entirely on the foundation of serving client needs.

Whenever I have spoken to groups of people about the JIT production system, someone invariably remarks, "You mean the Toyota *Kanban* System, right?" I suppose that is an indication of how famous the *kanban* system has become. The fact is, though, that the *kanban* system is part—but not all—of the JIT production system. The *kanban* system can be thought of as the conveyance system that helps make the JIT production system work. The JIT production system first gained public attention in Japan in the aftermath of the 1973 oil crisis, when market demand slacked off. A strong diversification trend was born, and Japan's economic growth slowed to a more modest rate. Amid this environment, the JIT production system gained the media notoriety as a recession-resistant production system.

The first aspect of the JIT production system to gain such attention was the *kanban* system, in which signs attached to goods replace vouchers as the medium for giving operating instructions and production orders.

JIT, or "Just-In-Time," refers to the timing of production flow; goods are delivered to the manufacturing lines just in time to be used, just in the immediately needed quantities, and just to the production processes that need them. Saying "in time" is not enough, since parts can arrive at processes a week or two prior to their use and still be there "in time."

That is why the most important word in Just-In-Time is the first word, "just." Goods need to arrive within minutes, not days or weeks, of their use on the production line. Only then can we eliminate waste in such forms as overproduction, waiting for late deliveries, and excess inventory.

Let's consider, for instance, a press operation. Imagine a big pile of cut sheet metal next to the press. All those sheets are there "in time" to be pressed. The sheet metal could have been cut yesterday and delivered "in time" to be pressed. Or it could have been cut and delivered last week or last month and still be there "in time." In any case, the sheet metal is there "in time" but not "just in time."

When the press operator is ready to press another sheet, all he needs is one sheet from the previous process. He does not need 10 or 20 of them. When he finishes pressing that one sheet, he is ready to get another one from the previous process. That is the way work-in-process should move, one at a time from the raw material stage to the finished product stage.

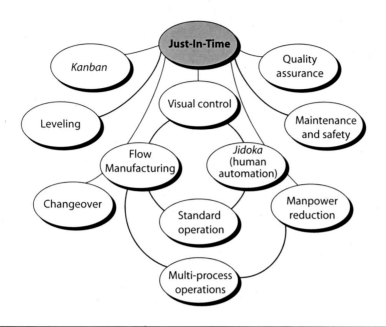

Figure 1.4   Overall Image of the JIT Production System.

It is helpful to picture Just-In-Time production as something like a river, in which separate workpieces float along in a level manner from station to station as they are sent downstream. Figure 1.4 presents an overall image of the JIT production system.

At first glance, the JIT production system seems simple enough, but when we begin to delve into its inner workings, we find it to be extremely complicated and full of things that cannot be well understood until they have been tried out in the factory. Factory-based improvements are not something to be talked about, written about, heard, or seen—they are something to be done. Such improvements are "hands-on" to their very core.

The following is an introduction to the types of improvements that must be made to bring about Just-In-Time production:

1. *Flow manufacturing*

   Flow manufacturing requires the elimination, whenever possible, of pile-ups and conveyances to enable work-in-process to flow in a level manner through the line. The goal is to have each workpiece move through the chain of processes so it is correctly processed within the cycle time.

2. *Multi-process handling*

In the conventional equipment layout scheme, where several machines having the same processing function are grouped together as a shop, one worker might be able to handle several machines, but handling several processes is out of the question. A different layout scheme, in which the machines that make up an entire sequence of processes are grouped together, would enable a single worker to move with the workpieces from process to process until the workpiece processing is finished. This latter arrangement is called multi-process handling.

3. *Kanban*

The *kanban* system comprises one of the tools for maintaining Just-In-Time production. *Kanban* are signs that contain operation instructions and/or parts delivery information. *Kanban* are useless in factories that still use the conventional "shish-kabob" type of production method. In fact, they tend to increase warehouse inventory levels in such situations. The factory must first switch over to flow manufacturing, and must start *pulling* workpieces from process to process rather than *pushing* them.

4. *Manpower reduction*

Conventionally, production lines have been organized with a view toward maintaining a steady number of workers on the line. The JIT production system rejects this way of thinking and instead organizes production using the minimum number of workers (personnel costs) required to meet the demand (fluctuation) of the next process (the market).

5. *Visual control*

A key method for making bold improvements is to make line failures or other factory-floor problems visible and obvious enough so that anyone can easily spot them. Various devices can be used to make production line problems more visible. *Kanban* and *andon* (line-stop alarm lights) are two such visual control devices.

6. *Leveling*

A little earlier, I used the term "shish-kabob" in discussing the kind of production scheme that was popular during the mass-production era. The shish-kabob image refers to the way that lots were processed in large, separate groups (the larger the better), much like the way meat and vegetables are set one by one on shish-kabob skewers. Lots were processed and then warehoused. The concept of leveling calls for product types and volumes to be spread out to produce as level a production flow as possible. Thus, leveling is fundamental to both Just-In-Time production and flow manufacturing.

7. *Changeover*

Here, I am using "changeover" as a broad term that covers not only the replacement of dies and blades, but also other operations, such as the revision of standards and the replacement of assembly parts and other materials. The goal of changeover improvements should be to shorten the time needed for such operations. They should make marked reductions in labor-hour requirements in order to build a strong, flexible manufacturing line that is adaptable to changes.

8. *Quality assurance*

Quality is not something that just happens when we have good production equipment. Likewise, having equipment operators work more cautiously does not necessarily reduce the number of defective products. Rather, quality assurance requires a comprehensive approach that addresses all production factors, including people, goods, production equipment, and production methods.

9. *Standard operations*

Standard operations are essential for maintaining flow manufacturing once it has been established and for keeping pace with the production schedule. In short, standard operations are the operations that have been painstakingly developed to achieve and preserve an effective combination of people, goods, and machines to produce high quality products economically, quickly, and safely.

10. *Jidoka: Human automation*

   Jidoka is automation with a human touch, and therefore differs from automation in the ordinary sense. *Jidoka* brings humans into the automation process to ensure reliability, flexibility, and precision.

11. *Maintenance and safety*

   In the JIT production system, the entire production flow is stopped whenever even the smallest machine breaks down. That is why the JIT production system places great value on maintenance activities that maintain high production capacity. Equal emphasis is placed on safety—the first and foremost consideration in production—in order to prevent breakdowns and accidents.

Introduction of the JIT Production System

Introduction Procedure

Adopting the JIT production system entails changing current production methods into JIT production methods. We generally refer to these kinds of changes as "JIT improvements."

   JIT improvements are quite different from the conventional industrial engineering (IE) type of factory improvements. The latter are usually based on analysis of current conditions. Improvement workers get out stopwatches and other instruments to measure current processes and then analyze them. Using the analysis results, they try to improve or fix the undesirable conditions.

   By contrast, JIT improvements are based on ideals instead of measurements. Their purpose is to bring the entire factory

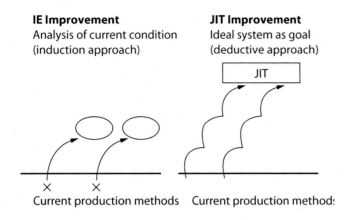

IE Improvement
Analysis of current condition
(induction approach)

JIT Improvement
Ideal system as goal
(deductive approach)

Current production methods   Current production method:

Figure 1.5   Improvement versus JIT Improvements.

into conformance with the requirements of the JIT production system. While IE improvements use an inductive approach based on statistical data, JIT improvements address a single issue—Just-In-Time production—and use a deductive approach to improve the factory (see Figure 1.5).

Rather than taking the slow plodding approach to fixing apparent problems within the current conditions, the JIT improvement approach moves by leaps and bounds to bring the factory as close as possible to the JIT model. As such, JIT improvement actually goes beyond "improvement" and into the realm of "innovation." Perhaps the term "JIT innovation" is more appropriate than "JIT improvement."

A factory cannot truly establish the JIT production system unless it successfully takes on all of the components of the overall JIT image that were shown in Figure 1.4. Figure 1.6 shows the five major steps in the upward sequence of events leading to success in establishing the JIT production system.

Step 1. The Awareness Revolution: Prerequisite for Factory Improvement

All innovation starts in the mind. Once we revolutionize our awareness of the factory situation, we will naturally want to improve the factory equipment and its layout and create better methods of operation. The JIT improvement concept does not mean going directly to the factory to make things

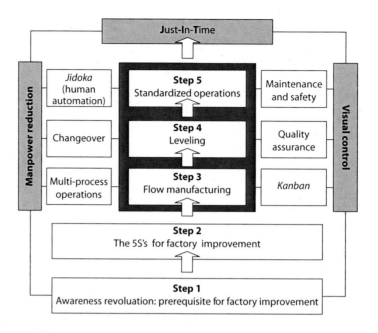

Figure 1.6   Steps in Establishing the JIT Production System.

better. Instead, the most important approach is to begin by revolutionizing people's awareness.

Manufacturing companies include all types of job functions, from business management to factory management, procurement, production, and so on. Production cannot proceed in a level manner unless all of these functions work well together on a day-to-day basis. And almost all of these functions are performed by people, not machines.

I am amazed at the kind of question I am asked when explaining this first step. For example, some people ask, "Who is supposed to revolutionize our awareness?" Others complain, "Hey, it's a production problem, so we've got to change the factory first."

I have even been told, "Look, the problems start with deliveries, and the buyers and subcontractors need to change first."

Right.

Obviously, it is important that everyone, including the production workers and the outside vendors, undergo the awareness revolution. But the best place to start is at the top. The reason for this is that as long as top management harbors such thoughts as, "There's no way to establish JIT with the way things are at this company," the necessary changes will not be made. You can bet on that.

When I hear such doubts coming from top managers, I always respond, "So, when are you going to get around to changing the way things are at your company?" Usually, they realize the futility of their thinking, and admit with a smile, "I guess we'll never have JIT unless we do something about it."

JIT improvement means more than changing production methods. Most companies are awash in problems arising from narrow self-interest or waste. Often, such problems have been around so long that they are unwittingly considered part of the "corporate culture."

The awareness revolution must start at the top of the company. There is no other way. Once top management people become more aware, they gain a heightened sense of what is wrong with the status quo. This sense of emergency begins to trickle down to middle management and then to the factory workers, until finally the whole company is filled with an awareness that things must change. It is this awareness that produces the energy needed to change the status quo. It creates a positive, dynamic force for change.

There are various ways to start and encourage this chain-reaction, such as holding in-house seminars and starting up JIT study groups to examine JIT movements and conditions in other manufacturing companies.

If only one thing sinks into the minds of all the company employees during these awareness revolution efforts, let it be that the status quo is not enough to ensure the company's survival in the future.

Step 2. The 5S's for Factory Improvement

Throughout the great effort to render the factory into a close approximation of the JIT model, we can look to five basic underlying principles. These principles are summarized by five words that, in romanized Japanese, begin with "S," and are thus called the 5S's. The 5S's are: proper arrangement (*seiri*), orderliness (*seiton*), cleanliness (*seiso*), cleanup (*seiketsu*), and discipline (*shitsuke*).

The most fundamental of these 5S basics are proper arrangement and orderliness. The success or failure to adhere to these two basics constitutes a major fork on the road to JIT success.

You are sure to find plenty of defective products when the factory is strewn with trash, when its floors and machines are oily or dusty, or when the production workers do not mind working in old, soiled uniforms. You will find plenty of late shipments, too. And low productivity. And low morale.

In any case, such factories are nowhere near being well-organized or well-regulated. Neither are they very neat or clean.

In Japan, about 70 percent of what we generally think of as factories are not factories. They are warehouses. The factory workers build things inside huge warehouses. They are surrounded by useless things and firmly plant themselves in front of unnecessary machines. Amid all this clutter, the workers literally go out of their way to make things. Often, workers must waste time looking for things that they need, such as parts, dies, or tools. The workers that have been there long enough to have figured out where those things are likely to be are called "veterans."

Under such conditions, there is really nowhere to begin making JIT improvements. First, we have to go back to the most basic of the 5S's, proper arrangement and orderliness. To do this, we begin figuring out exactly what and how much is really needed in the factory.

Putting up a big sign emblazoned with the words "Proper Arrangement and Orderliness" is obviously not going to do the trick if the floor is still cluttered with unnecessary parts and assorted garbage. Improvements do not come from banners. Neither do they flow from the mouths of pep-talkers. Improvements are things that get done on the spot.

Two of the biggest obstacles for proper arrangement and orderliness are poor training and ignorance of proper methods. The most effective way to bring about proper arrangement and orderliness is to keep things visible. When trying out a new arrangement plan, a 5-year-old child should be able to figure out what is necessary and what is not. Once it is decided where things should go and in what quantities, any amateur—whether a company president or a visitor—should be able to easily recognize the rules.

This is what is meant by "visual proper arrangement and orderliness." The strategy for bringing about visual proper arrangement is called "the red tag strategy." The strategy for establishing visual orderliness is called "the *kanban* strategy."

When carrying out the red tag strategy, the company forms red tag teams to perform company-wide red tag campaigns from two to four times over the span of a year. It is vital that the red tag strategy be maintained for at least a year, or else the company will likely slip back into its old sloppy habits.

Step 3. Flow Manufacturing

Whenever I am asked what flow manufacturing means, I always respond, "It means bringing the factory's underlying waste to the surface."

Whether the production method is shish-kabob production or one-piece flow manufacturing, the product is the same. One might think that since the end product is the same, it does not matter which method is used.

However, there is one important difference here. Shish-kabob production tends to conceal waste while flow manufacturing tends to reveal it. That is the only significant difference between the two methods. For beginners looking to make JIT improvements, it is still much too early to think about what differences there are between the two methods when applying them to such matters as greatly improving productivity and more readily meeting customer needs.

Shish-kabob production of large lots was fine during the bygone era of fast-expanding sales. Companies grew larger without regard to how much "fat" or waste they were accumulating. In the seller's market of those days, the manufacturer's waste-related costs could just be added into the product's marketable price.

Now it is a buyer's market. Today's buyers do not need or wish to subsidize manufacturers' waste-related costs. In fact, nowadays consumers are smart enough to lay the blame for such waste-related costs directly on the manufacturer.

Unfortunately, waste usually runs deep within any factory. And deeply embedded waste is not at all easy to discover. Such waste has, in a sense, spread roots. Like real roots, the roots of waste sometimes get severed when you try to pull them out, and you have to go deeper to get the rest of them, or they will grow back later. Waste has to be eradicated completely. Small-scale improvements will not do the job.

Now let's get on to how flow manufacturing is employed.

Manufacturing products one at a time allows us to look right into the depths of how the products are made. All of the major and minor forms of waste that had been concealed by the large-lot shish-kabob production method are now visible.

We begin to notice odd things and ask questions like:

- "Why are we conveying the workpiece from here to there?"
- "Why are the parts piling up right here?"
- "Why does changeover have to take so long?"

Setting up for flow manufacturing is a piece of cake. There are only seven requirements, as listed in Figure 1.7. If all seven are met, the factory will have bona fide flow manufacturing. It is as simple as that.

I doubt that the novice at JIT improvement would understand what any of these tersely worded requirements mean. Below is a more detailed description of each.

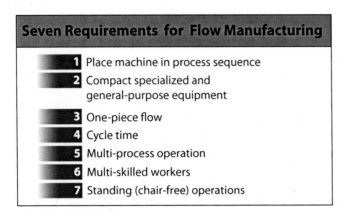

Figure 1.7   Seven Requirements for Flow Manufacturing.

1. *Continuous flow production line*

   This means arranging the production processes (and the production equipment) into a line or a U-shaped cell.

2. *Compact specialized and general-purpose equipment*

   Costs can be kept down by installing smaller, slower, and more specialized production equipment. However, some general-purpose equipment is also needed to facilitate flexible line reorganization.

3. *One-piece flow*

   This means that each process should handle only one workpiece unit from the time processing of that work-piece is begun until it is finished.

4. *Cycle time*

   This refers to the need to synchronize processes to keep pace with client needs and the needs of the next process.

5. *Multi-process handling*

   This is a labor arrangement in which one worker moves from process to process down the line.

6. *Multi-skilled workers*

   This entails training workers in the skills needed for multi-process handling.

7. *Standing (chair-free) operations*

   An important improvement in work posture is changing from sitting to standing, enabling worker mobility.

Step 4. Leveling

In principle, it is best to start JIT improvements as close as possible to the client. In the factory, that would mean starting by reducing finished product warehouse inventories to zero. If we can tear down the wall of piled-up products that need to be shipped and sold, we are better able to incorporate the latest client needs into the factory. Those product "walls" protect factories from the powerful waves of changing client needs. They give the factories a false sense of security, especially today when factories need to remain in intimate touch with market trends.

It is only by tearing down those walls that factories can come face to face with the needs of today's market for greater diversification and shorter lead-times. Factories may then promptly change their production lines to reflect those needs.

Then, as the old QC saying goes, "the next process is your customer." After aiming to meet client needs for a certain product, JIT improvements move on to the product's sub-assembly lines, processing lines, materials processing lines, and outside orders. (See Figure 1.8.) This is called "vertical development" of JIT improvements. We call it "lateral development" when JIT improvement moves on to other products.

Therefore, as a rule, JIT improvement begins near the client and moves upstream from the "next process" to the "prior process."

To recapitulate, to start off the JIT improvement campaign, we get rid of the stacks of finished products in the warehouse and then we change the final assembly processes to suit the client's current needs. To do this, we must put an end to the factory's shish-kabob style of lot production. The factory is no longer going to turn out large lots of product A this week and large lots of product B next week. That is not the way customers buy things. It is only the way that seems most convenient for the factory.

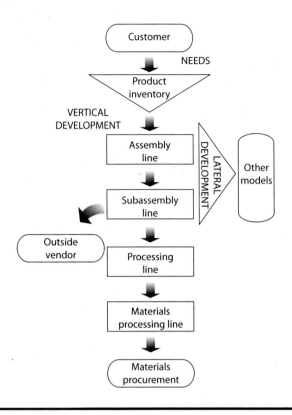

Figure 1.8   Sequence for Introducing JIT Improvement.

Although the exact quantities of each product fluctuate a little, customers invariably buy a wide range of products. Bringing such diversity into the production system is what we mean by "production leveling."

Many people think of production leveling as leveling out two factors: capacity and load. System engineers who work with computer-based production control systems are especially quick to make this association. They think in terms of the various processes' capacities and the load that production orders impose on those processes. So when the load piles up to where it exceeds the capacity, the load "peaks" need to be leveled out.

But three things are clearly wrong about the load and capacity approaches to production leveling.

Let us address the first of this approach's problems by asking, "Who determines what a process's load is anyway?" The factory does, and usually for reasons of convenience.

This is the first mistake. The factory people are saying this is their capacity, regardless of what the client requires. They need to stand that approach on its head and make the client's needs the factor that determines the capacity.

The second mistake is to break up the load of orders from customers once that load exceeds the predetermined capacity. Orders from customers should be treated with more respect than that. Instead of breaking up the load and thereby lengthening lead-time, the factory should pursue other options, such as temporary overtime work or subcontracting.

The third mistake in this approach is that it relies on people who sit at their desks with pen, paper, and calculator or computer and plan production schedules, but do not know how to make the products. It is the old ivory tower syndrome. The farther production planners are from the production line, the more impractical their planning becomes. Instead of working out uselessly detailed production plans, they need to plan directly for client needs. The simple way is the best way.

For JIT improvement, leveling means thoroughly leveling out product types and volumes in accordance with customer needs. In other words, we begin by breaking down the monthly production output into daily units. Then we compare the daily volume of products with the operating hours and calculate how many minutes it should take to turn out each product unit. We call this unit production time "cycle time." Then we figure out how many people are needed and what the capacity is (see Figure 1.9). Naturally, this requires organizing manpower based on the production lines instead of organizing production lines based on a fixed number of workers.

It is all too easy to find factories that calculate such things as production capacity and production line speed based on the equipment or the maximum number of worker hours. That approach is fundamentally wrong. It bears repeating that it is the customer—not the factory—who should determine how many products are to be made and how quickly. This fact must never be forgotten.

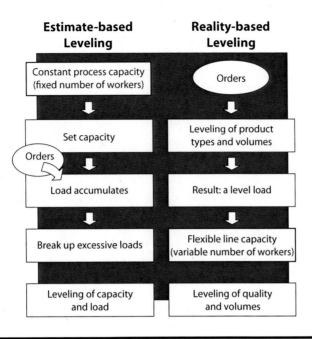

Figure 1.9   Estimate-Based Leveling and Reality-Based Leveling.

Step 5. Standard Operations

It so happens that many of the important elements we work with in factories begin with the letter "M": manpower, materials, machines, methods (such as work methods), and money (economics).

Standard operations are those operations which have been determined as best achieving and preserving an effective combination of people, goods, and machines in order to produce high-quality products economically, quickly, and safely.

Again, we must deal with a common misconception. Many people mistakenly think of standard operations as being the same as standard operating procedures (SOPs). The difference is that SOPs are only standards for individual operations; they are merely part of what we mean by standard operations.

Standard operations are standards that string together a series of operation-specific SOPs in a particular order to build a certain product. As such, they are more like "standard production procedures" than standard operating procedures.

In addition, standardized work procedures serve a dual purpose. They not only help standardize production, but they also help reveal current operating conditions. In view of this dual purpose, the proper way to establish standardized work procedures is to follow the steps listed below.

Step 1: Reveal current operating conditions. The first thing to do is to discover and analyze the actual net time currently required for work operations and the way in which operations are really being performed.

Step 2: Ferret out the problems. Use the cycle time as a standard for ferreting out problems regarding the work balance, ergonomic factors, variation, and so on.

Step 3: Find out the real causes and plan improvement. Repeatedly ask "Why?" along with other key questions (the "5 Whys and 1 How") until you discover the real cause of the problem, then plan out an improvement to resolve it.

Step 4: Implement the improvement. Go into the factory and implement whatever improvements are needed concerning operations, hardware, layout, and the like.

Step 5: Standard operations. Once you have improved the operations, establish them officially as standardized work procedures, which will again come under scrutiny during the next improvement stage.

From Vertical Development to Horizontal Development

The first two steps in introducing the JIT production system, the awareness revolution and the 5S's, should be developed throughout the factory and/or company. Obviously, the 5S's step will not work unless the awareness revolution step has been taken. The company is not ready to begin the second step until the awareness revolution has taken root, at least to some extent.

Once the awareness revolution and the 5S's have thoroughly penetrated the factory, JIT improvements can begin.

These improvements begin with what is most obvious and expand from single improvement points to "lines," and finally to "planes" and "cubes." Below are descriptions of each expansion phase.

Point Improvements

Even Just-In-Time improvements cannot begin with flow manufacturing. Instead, they must begin with a rooting out of the basic causes of workpiece pile-ups at certain processes and a change in production methods to eliminate the need for product warehouses. We must ask the basic question "Why?" at each point where workpieces are being conveyed between processes, to find out whether such conveyance can be eliminated. We must observe each worker's movements and see if they can be made simpler, more efficient, and less wasteful.

These are all "point" improvements. Like seeds planted in furrows, these small point improvements must be carried out as a foundation to support larger improvements later on. (See Figure 1.10.)

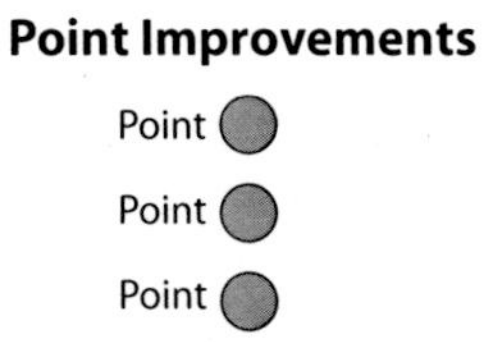

Point Improvements

Point ⬤
Point ⬤
Point ⬤

Figure 1.10   Point Improvements.

Line Improvements

After accumulating a certain amount of point improvements aimed at workpiece pile-ups, wasteful conveyance, and the like, we reach a breakthrough point where suddenly things begin to flow. Such a phenomenon indicates that enough point improvements have been made in the factory to pave the way for some line improvements. From a technical viewpoint, this is where flow manufacturing begins.

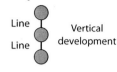

Line Improvements

Figure 1.11   Line Improvements.

Once we start making line improvements in the factory, it is time to change the production method from "push" production to "pull" production, plan for production leveling, and develop standard operations. It is also important that we move promptly to make improvements whenever problems occur in the flow of work-in-process and that we practice "visual control." These are the kinds of activities I call "line improvements."

Line improvements always occur as the result of an accumulation of point improvements. There is no sense in trying to force a quantum jump to line improvements without any foundation. Neither is it wise to try to use rigid rules for drawing a straight line from one desired improvement to the next. But we need at least to understand the line's starting and ending points in order to know what kind of line we are drawing. This kind of drawing between points is called "vertical development." (See Figure 1.11.)

We generally use this kind of vertical development to build model lines. Model lines can be selected for a particular type of production line segment or for a particular type of product. In either case, the person in charge of the model line must be someone who is really enthusiastic and eager to do a good job.

Plane Improvements

Once we have vertically developed improvements on our model line at the selected production line segment, we are ready to display the model line to people at other processes to use as a reference for carrying out their own point and line improvements. This way, a single line improvement at

Plane Improvements

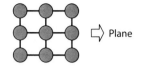

Figure 1.12   Plane Improvements.

one part of the factory floor becomes two and then three lines at various other parts until, finally, the whole factory floor has been improved. This is "plane improvement." We also call this type of follow-the-model improvement "lateral development," as illustrated in Figure 1.12.

Cube Improvements

Product manufacturing cannot be done well by a factory alone. The factory needs market information from the company's sales arm and component deliveries from buyers and outside vendors. It also needs a distribution organization to deliver the finished products to market.

Once the circle of JIT improvement has expanded to where it encloses the entire factory, it can be gradually raised to other "planes" outside of the factory. In this way, plane improvements become "cube improvements." (See Figure 1.13.)

Cube Improvements

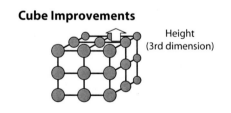

Figure 1.13   Cube Improvements.

Organizing for JIT Introduction

JIT production is an "industrial revolution" that aids corporate survival and helps revolutionize employee awareness. This means that JIT production is a form of innovation, and innovation requires casting away fixed ideas and old habits.

As such, JIT introduction is not something we can do in our spare time. It is a major undertaking, and to get substantial results it desperately needs the support of top managers cheering, "Let's get to it!" and factory floor leaders urging, "Let's move this thing forward!"

The entire company has to get behind JIT introduction as a sort of company-wide "JIT Improvement Project." Figure 1.14 illustrates the method for promoting company-wide involvement in JIT introduction.

JIT improvements are neither academic accomplishments nor problem-hunting tours of the factory by the technical staff. As shown in Figure 1.14, they are nuts-and-bolts changes that work their way through the entire production organization to improve the factory.

Such improvement organizations for JIT production cannot succeed unless everyone carries out his or her duties seriously and enthusiastically.

- *The president's duties: Company-wide reinforcement of JIT production.*

  Just-In-Time includes more than production. JIT must also be extended to all other arms of the company, such as sales, procurement, subcontractors, distributors, and so on.

- *Duties of the factory superintendents, division chiefs, and department chiefs: Establishment and company-wide achievement of goals for JIT production.*

  Most factories run on an internal organization that has evolved and developed over many years. That is why two factories that belong to the same company may be quite different from one another. Faced with such long-cultivated traditions, JIT improvements cannot succeed unless the factory management—including the supervisor, division chiefs, and department chiefs—all get involved. It is especially important that they get involved

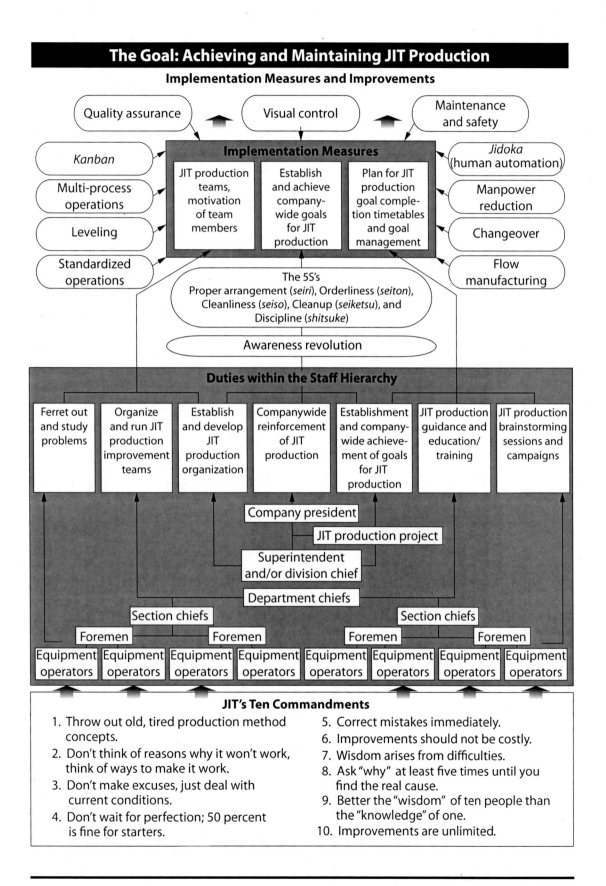

Figure 1.14 Promotion of Company-wide JIT Production.

in such things as improvement follow-ups and ensuring the thorough implementation of JIT production.

■ *Duties of department chiefs and section chiefs: Giving guidance, education and training in JIT production, and creation and management of JIT improvement teams.*

Even within the same factory, we often find that JIT improvements reach different degrees of advancement in different departments. When advancement is poor, much of the blame can be placed at the feet of the department chief and the section chiefs. An unenthusiastic department chief alone is often enough to slow progress. Or perhaps the section chiefs are just following orders and have no real interest in what they are doing. Successful JIT promotion groups include department and section chiefs whose enthusiasm attracts the interested participation of the foremen and equipment operators.

■ *Duties of section chiefs, foremen, and equipment operators: Gaining hands-on experience in JIT production and ferreting out and studying problems.*

The foremen and equipment operators are the ones who best understand how the factory works. By the same token, they are the ones who tend to be most reluctant to discard the traditional way of doing things. Therefore, they need to gain a great deal of courage and fervor to overcome such reluctance. They need to be convinced that there is no use complaining about the changes. There is, on the other hand, every reason to push forward to make the improvements.

Figure 1.15 shows an example of how one company set-up its promotional organization.

How to Promote and Carry Out JIT Improvements

Once we have set-up an organization for introducing JIT production, we are ready to begin improvement activities.

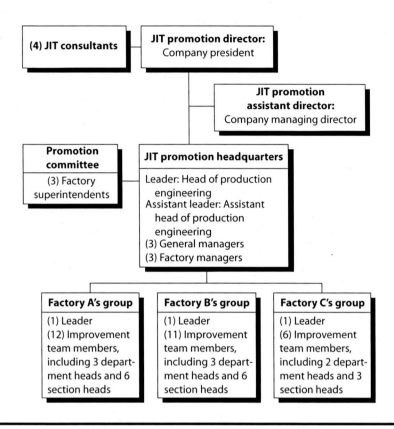

Figure 1.15   Example of Promotional Organization for JIT Production.

However, these are not improvements in the ordinary sense of the word. Instead, the factory is looked at as a dynamic system, and improvements made as if to a living entity.

Conventionally, small improvements in the factory occur every day and have an accumulative effect. In factories where improvement activities are assigned only to a certain group (or even just one person), improvements can still be accumulated, but it is a very difficult task. That is why the factory needs a company-wide promotional organization.

In addition, there are five key points to observe in introducing JIT improvement activities.

Point 1. Set-Up an Improvement Promotion Office

Set aside an empty room in the factory. The room should be large enough for about ten people, or however many are on the improvement project team. This is the room where improvement teams can come to work out an agenda of problems and brainstorm corrective measures. The room should never be used as a recreation room.

The improvement teams should meet here one day a week to study improvement issues. The other days they should be busy carrying out improvements.

Point 2. Have at Least One "Improvement Day" a Week

For all improvement project members, the cycle of improvement meetings and activities should be at least weekly. Do not let people get the idea that they should only be making improvements on the day meetings are held. On nonmeetings days, people in every part of the factory should be busy carrying out improvement measures.

"Improvement Day" activities should also include progress reports on current improvement campaigns, brainstorming for new improvement points, and assignment of improvement activity duties.

Point 3. Improvement Meetings: One Hour Is Better Than Two Hours

Improvement meetings are not the goal of JIT improvements. The first and foremost goal is to make the necessary changes to create a factory that effectively responds to market needs. Just sitting at a desk and talking about improvements is not going to change anything.

Therefore, the meetings should be short and to the point. We simply figure out the key agenda items, brainstorm improvement ideas, assign improvement jobs, set a delivery deadline, then get back to the factory to start making the improvements. We should try to finish the meeting within an hour, or within two hours at the most.

When scheduling the meetings, be sure to avoid meal times when people need to eat. Eating is important to labor productivity. The best time for improvement meetings (Figure 1.16) is usually in the evening, right after work.

Figure 1.16 An Improvement Meeting.

Point 4. Create an Improvement List

During a one-hour walk through the factory, any sharp-eyed observer can usually spot ten to 15 items in need of improvement. All items should be entered on an improvement list to be used for proposing improvement ideas at weekly improvement meetings.

The items do not have to be typed. The list can be on a blackboard or poster on the wall of the improvement promotion office, where people can casually jot down things they have noticed. However, the list should contain columns with the following headings to enhance clarity:

1. Improvement number
2. Improvement item name
3. Description of improvement
4. Related section/department
5. Improvement leader
6. Delivery deadline
7. Result

Because this list will be used for making improvements, it is important that every column be filled in to keep the status and progress of improvements as clearly visible as possible. It is the responsibility of the improvement project leaders to check the

"Result" column at each meeting to gauge the overall progress of improvement activities.

Point 5. Improvements Happen in the Factory!

Improvement meetings are basically for confirming the previous week's improvement campaigns and assigning duties for the next week's campaign. After that, it is time to get back to the factory where improvements actually happen.

Once the meeting is over, the various improvement teams—such as the equipment layout team, jig redesign team, and 5S's enforcement team—should go directly to the places in the factory where the improvements are to be made. The improvement teams may be there until late in the evening, but when they finish, they will get a sense of real achievement. Making improvements cannot be done halfheartedly or left half done. A "hang in there" attitude must be maintained until the end.

Chapter 2

Destroying Factory Myths
A Revolutionary Approach

Relations among Sales Price, Cost, and Profit

1. Costs + profits = sales price
2. Sales price – profits = costs

What do you notice when you look at these two equations? If you get the impression that they say the same thing, you have a knack for math. Mathematically, there is no difference between the two equations. However, if you are a business manager or someone fluent in finance concepts, you would recognize the equation's algebraic similarity, but you would also insist that they are two completely different ways of thinking.

How can we explain this?

In the first equation—*costs + profits = sales price*—the method for determining the sales price is to add a profit margin onto costs. Specifically, we first identify and add up all the costs involved in manufacturing a planned commercial product. Then we tack on a profit margin to reach a sales price. We can call this the "cost up" method.

The second equation—*sales price – profits = costs*—sets the sales price according to the market price.

To do this, we first find out how much the planned product will likely fetch on the market and take that value as the sales price. Then we need to decide how big a profit margin is required. The total costs are what is left over when we subtract the profit from the sales (market) price.

After that, we can go on to ask questions like, "What kind of materials can we use and still keep the costs within the equation's total cost figure?" We can also work out our choices of production methods and labor resources in this way.

The *costs + profit = sales price* approach is based on predetermined costs, and is therefore a production-oriented approach. In Japan, the latest jargon describes this as the "product-out" approach.

On the other hand, the *sales price − profit = costs* approach takes the opposite direction by starting with the market as a base. It is therefore a market-oriented (or "market-in") approach.

Which approach do you think is better suited to today's highly competitive markets? In a mature market, the product-oriented approach will only work for an extraordinarily popular and distinctive product. Otherwise, the product would be outsold by similar products whose prices follow downward moving market trends. In addition, we should not regard profit as a side product. Instead of being pleasantly surprised by the appearance of a profit, we should take more positive steps to ensure one.

The sales price is almost always being pushed downward by market needs. That leaves only one viable method for squeezing a profit out of the equation: lowering costs.

In recent years, the companies that have been the biggest profit-earners are the ones that have been best able to keep costs down. The losers have been those that have not been able to cut costs. You cannot blame many of the losers for not trying. Many have tried Total Quality Control (TQC), cost reduction projects, suggestion systems, small group activities, and various types of employee committees, but none of these have been thorough enough to bring real success.

Many of the losers in today's tough markets have been companies that sincerely pulled together in pursuit of certain goals. The problem for them has been the same old story: the attitudes of employees, many of whom lack the confidence or courage to reach the goals. Employees who think of what they cannot do instead of simply planning the next step ahead are the root of these failures. The key word here is "innovation." Companies that forget that word are just biding their time until bankruptcy.

Another key concept is that profit is not something that "pops out" of the manufacturing and marketing processes and lands in the laps of the company employees. Rather, it is something the company has to create and earn through hard work.

Companies have to take a more positive attitude toward profit-earning. They have to be creative and come up with devices and schemes that will help create profit. The way to start is to *throw out every single conventional idea.* The factory's local mythology—the proud tales of how many years the factory has been turning out good old Product X—has to be discarded and replaced by a cold, hard look at market needs.

Some companies have been able to do this, and some have not. Some just do not have the inner strength for it. Let us briefly examine what the anatomy of an unprofitable factory might look like, as illustrated in Figure 2.1.

In this example, the company figures its sales price using the production-oriented method, and then launches its sales activities. However, the actual costs turn out to be much more than the original estimate. This shrinks the profit to a modest or very small amount. Unless the factory can recover its profitability, morale will start to sink.

Some belt-tightening is needed, and such things as R&D and improvement campaigns are the first to go. Soon the factory falls into the bad habit of slashing precisely the programs that might alleviate the problem. Such short-sightedness ends up creating a genuinely unprofitable factory.

Now let us compare this money-losing factory to the one whose anatomy is shown in Figure 2.2.

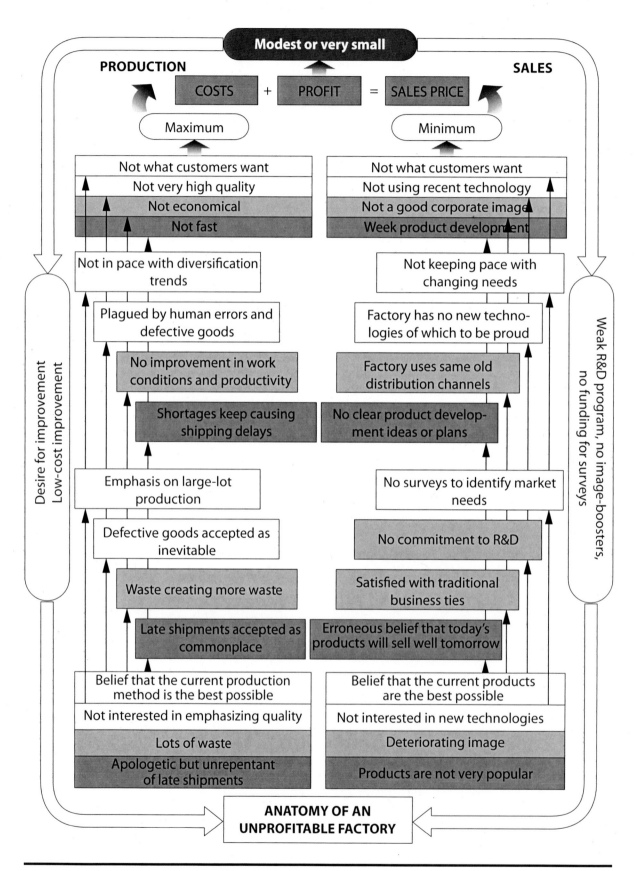

Figure 2.1   Anatomy of an Unprofitable Factory.

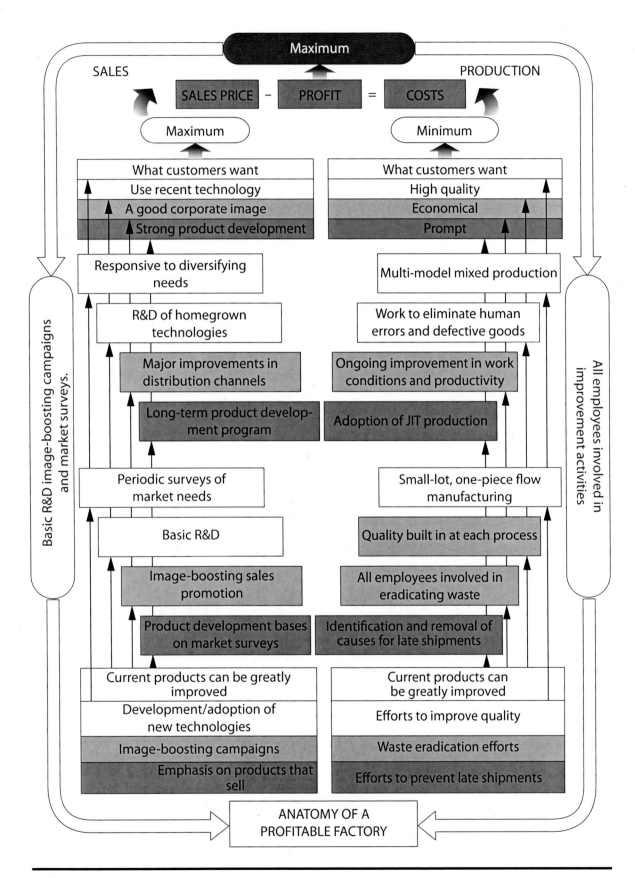

Figure 2.2   Anatomy of a Profitable Factory.

As can be seen, anatomically speaking, these two factories are almost complete opposites. In the latter case, the sales price is set according to the "going price" on the market.

The company's sales division is busy carrying out energetic marketing activities in sales promotion, distribution channels, and other areas. Meanwhile, all of the employees in the production division are equally busy with broad-reaching efforts to completely eliminate human errors, product defects, and waste. As a result, the company is able to maintain sales, suppress costs, and turn a good profit.

When profits rise, so does employee morale. In addition, management is more willing to underwrite such initiatives as R&D, sales promotions, plant investment, and improvement activities.

Here we have an example of a profitable factory, fueled by innovation. And remember, innovation is the key to success.

Ten Arguments against the JIT Production Revolution

People naturally tend to harbor a mild affinity toward one another. Co-workers tend to harbor a very strong affinity with their system of "the way things are done," which they have built together over the years. As far as they are concerned, no system could be better for them. They have no desire to change it. After all, their routine is leveled and is very easy to live with. Even in the finest-looking factories, life goes on in the traditional, albeit obsolete, manner.

Improvement starts at the factory:

"Hey Joey, could you roll that set of machines over here? I want to link them up with this process."
"Hey, no way. Why all the hassle?"
"Haven't you heard? We're dropping this lot production stuff and gearing up for one-piece flow."

Ten Arguments Against JIT Improvement

1. JIT improvements won't do any good!
2. It sounds like a good thing, but we still don't want to do it!
3. Looks good on paper, but . . .
4. Costs are already as low as that can possibly get!
5. But we've already been doing things that way!
6. We don't want people looking over our shoulders and telling us what to do!
7. We can't lower costs any more without lowering quality!
8. Everything is going just fine now. Why change it!
9. That's a lousy idea! We already tried that 20 years ago!
10. Look, we understand this stuff better than anybody (so don't tell us what to do).

Figure 2.3   Ten Arguments against JIT Improvement.

"Do you have any idea what kind of quality problems these changes are going to create?"

"Come on, move it. I want you to have this set-up for one-piece production before I come by again."

"If you say so, but it won't work."

The three common excuses encountered at this point boil down to: "I don't want to change things," "It's too much trouble," and, "I'm afraid I'll get laid off."

Aside from these common excuses, I have been able to identify ten arguments against JIT that are often encountered on the path of JIT improvement. Figure 2.3 lists these arguments.

These are just some of the wide variety of anti-JIT arguments one runs into when trying to promote JIT improvements.

To elaborate a bit:

1. *"JIT improvements won't do any good!"*

Here we have a sweeping condemnation of the whole JIT improvement program.

2. *"It sounds like a good thing, but we still don't want to do it!"* and

3. *"Looks good on paper, but..."*

Here we have agreement in general and disagreement on all particulars.

4. *"Costs are already as low as they can possibly get!"* and

5. *"We can't lower costs any more without lowering quality!"*

Here the obstacle is the fixed idea that costs are already at their minimum.

6. *"But we've already been doing things that way!"*

7. *"We don't want people looking over our shoulders and telling us what to do!"* and

8. *"Everything is going just fine now. Why change it?"*

Here we have a general reluctance to change the status quo. This is very common among workers in factories that are still managing to turn some kind of profit.

9. *"That's a lousy idea! We already tried that 20 years ago!"* and

10. *"Look, we understand this stuff better than anybody (so don't tell us what to do)."*

Finally, here we have the kind of resistance that is born out of cockiness and defensiveness.

Alas, JIT means having to deal with all kinds of people and their reluctance to change. JIT improvement has tended to stir up the same old resistance that has arisen many times in the past. Many years ago, General Electric ran into the same kind of resistance when it was making big changes with VA/VE programs.

Innovations come in waves. Each time a new wave of innovation comes roaring in, the environment must be flexible enough to adapt to it. People are innately tough customers when it comes to buying ideas that threaten the status quo. And in factories, the word "change" is virtually taboo.

Nevertheless, JIT improvement requires that all fixed ideas be cast aside so a new consciousness suitable for the new environment may be cultivated. Achieving this task takes much longer than merely improving operations or equipment. It demands that the very same things be done again and again.

From the company president down to the factory workers, the subject of improvement has to be openly discussed. During such discussions, we are bound to run into negative comments, such as, "There's no way that JIT stuff is going to work in our factory."

There is also the idea that the people responsible for JIT improvement are not qualified for the job. In such cases, they can prove their point by asking the disgruntled factory people a few pointed questions, such as:

"Look at your factory. Defects are out of control, shipments are always late, and warehouse inventory seems to have no limit. What are you going to do about it? What specific plans do you have to solve these problems?"

The response to that is usually dead silence. Sometimes, you have to challenge fixed ideas directly.

People are not going to unleash themselves from their gut feelings of resistance and their fixed ideas unless they are instilled with the basic spirit of improvement. Figure 2.4 shows a policy statement illustrating this basic spirit at a kitchenware company. Figure 2.5 shows a manifestation of this spirit at a fishing equipment manufacturer.

These signboards usually measure about one square meter and are made of vellum. They can be either hung from ceilings or posted on walls. It is a good idea to display these signboards not only in management meeting rooms, but also

---

Statement of Basic Spirit

1 Let's throw out the "how-to" habits (the factory's myths)!
2 Don't try to explain why it won't work, think of a way to make it work!
3 Instead of making excuses, make the current situation different!
4 Immediately start doing what is right and stop doing what is wrong!
5 Don't wait for the perfect plan; 60 percent is better than nothing!
6 Fix mistakes right then and there!
7 Wisdom grows out of difficulties!
8 Ask "Why?" at least five times to find the true cause! Then find out "How" to make the improvement! Remember the five W's and one H!
9 Ten wise men are better than one whiz kid.
10 **Improvements are unlimited!**

Figure 2.4   Basic Spirit of Improvement at a Kitchenware Company.

in factory meeting rooms and at various processes along the production lines.

This way, whenever someone starts griping, "We can't do that," we can save our breath and just point at the sign.

These signboard statements of the "basic spirit" for improvement can serve as bold reminders for workers who have forgotten what the basic spirit is all about.

If not out of sight, the "basic spirit" is less likely to be kept out of mind.

Approach to Production as a Whole

Fixed Ideas and the JIT Production Approach

In most factories, fixed ideas about how things should be manufactured are unwittingly created over the years. The fact that they get created is bad enough. Worse still is the fact that they are quickly adopted as the gospel truth.

In other words, such fixed ideas are developed into a local "mythology" at each factory, and the factory's inhabitants are

O-N-P Basic Spirit

1 Do it now!

2 No excuses!

3 Make the forms we need!

4 Bring the top managers into the factory to check out the problems!

5 Destroy the myths!

6 Improvements are unlimited!

7 Things can only get better than they are now!

8 Don't wait for the perfect plan. Getting at least halfway there is better than not trying.

9 Ask "Why?" at least five times to find the true cause!

10 Fix mistakes right then and there!

11 Don't waste time thinking about it—do it!

12 Finish what you start!

13 Don't let worries slow you down!

14 Don't waste energy thinking of reasons why it won't work. Think instead of ways to make it work.

15 Wisdom arises from difficulties!

16 Don't throw money at problems, use your brains! And if your brains aren't enough, use your sweat!

17 You won't have the ability to do it until you have the mind to do it!

18 Constant "fine-tuning" of equipment is not a good thing—it means operators are covering up for faulty engineering.

19 Constant money will not produce more money!

20 Those who do not want to do the job are not fit for the job!

21 Lot sizes show how strong the company is!

22 Ignore any orders without a deadline!

Figure 2.5   Policy Statement at a Fishing Equipment Company.

naturally suspicious of anything that threatens to desecrate such sacred lore as the following.

> "Economy means economy of scale: Lot sizes must be at least 1,000 units."
>
> "Fine-tuning the dies is how a die press operator shows his skill."
>
> "Sampling inspection is the most intelligent way to find defects."
>
> "Stand to work? You must be kidding! This work takes precision handwork, and you've got to sit down to do that."
>
> "I've been working here for 20 years and I've already figured out the best way to do this job."

I could go on for pages and pages with more of these "myths." There seems to be an inexhaustible supply of "why it's got to be done this way" myths at every factory.

The people who still subscribe to these myths have little idea how outdated they became when the "whatever you make will sell" era came to a close. They may hear consumers complain, but they don't really listen to the complaints and think about them.

It is amazing how many factories are still like that.

When visiting such factories to discuss the JIT production system, I have sometimes gotten the impression that introducing JIT improvement programs at factories so firmly rooted in shish-kabob production is like praying to a horse or giving a penny to a cat.

As I said earlier, we have to begin with the awareness revolution. It is a good idea to somehow make the need for a change in consciousness a topic on everyone's mind at both the start and end of the workday routine. It is also a good idea to make the adoption of the JIT production system a theme for QC circles and other small group activities. Another effective device is to invite outside experts to give employee seminars.

If the 5S's are the foundation for improving the factory, then we could say that the awareness revolution is the premise for JIT production. If we can change people's minds, we can do anything.

JIT production system concepts should be used to overhaul conventional thinking and cannot simply be used to supplement the old philosophy. Hard as this is, JIT awareness revolution means discarding work methods that are the result of years of study and experience, and long-accumulated know-how. It even goes beyond that and requires everyone to consider the present way of doing things as the worst possible way.

The kind of "improvements" called for by the JIT production system are not the easy kind of minor improvements that make current conditions a little bit better. JIT improvements begin in the mind, expand to every corner of the factory, and take root to radically change the factory. They do not simply make the current situation a little better. Each JIT improvement is an innovation, a revolutionary advancement that introduces a whole new concept and methodology. It is probably more correct to describe the activity of JIT improvements as "revolutionizing the factory" rather than merely improving it.

Likewise, a JIT awareness revolution does not just improve our ideas about manufacturing systems—it introduces revolutionary, boldly innovative ideas.

Lesson 1. JIT Means Innovation

"Just-In-Time"

To put it briefly, Just-In-Time means manufacturing and procuring "just what is needed, just when it is needed, and just in the amount needed." The Just-In-Time concept must be applied not only to manufacturing, but to all other aspects of the business, including subcontracting, procurement, and distribution.

As mentioned earlier, Just-In-Time tends to be interpreted as meaning "in time," which is quite wrong.

The "In Time" concept is already fairly well observed in factories everywhere. After all, a factory cannot function unless its buyers and subcontractors deliver their goods in time for them to be used in the factory. Similarly, a downstream process cannot operate on workpieces until the workpieces have been finished at the previous upstream process.

Outside vendors and subcontractors all have deadlines for the products they deliver to specific processes in the client factory. These deadlines are extended down the line as a delivery deadline for product shipment to sales firms, and then as the sales firms' delivery deadline for shipment to customers.

If we think of Just-In-Time as simply beating the delivery deadline, we understand very little of what JIT is all about.

Beating the delivery deadline is what "in time" means. Just-In-Time means something quite different.

Let us suppose next Friday is our delivery deadline date. The In Time concept interprets this as meaning we need to deliver our products by next Friday. We could deliver them next Thursday if we wish. We could even deliver them on Monday. Or, if they are ready now, we could send them over immediately and not even wait for next week.

The same principle can be seen at work within factories. For instance, next to the press machine there might be a large pile of workpieces that has been sent down from the previous process. The In Time concept says that is OK. In fact, though, the workpieces are a little *too much in time*.

Compare that with an example in which the press operator calls out "Ready!" and immediately receives a single workpiece from the previous process. He presses it, then calls out "Ready!" again and receives another workpiece. Here we have a manifestation of the Just-In-Time concept.

But even when we add the term "just" to "in time," we still are not saying half of what Just-In-Time really means.

This is because the JIT production system is more than just a new production method and production system for maintaining delivery deadlines, building things in small production runs, and so on. It is also a technique for thoroughly eradicating waste by rooting out deep-seated waste wherever it exists in the company—in both factories and offices—and using JIT improvements to eliminate the waste.

Let us consider for a moment just how thorough this eradication of waste under the "Just" concept really is.

For example, if we interpret the "just" in Just-In-Time as meaning "about one month," that means the factory is allowed to operate with one month of inventory-related waste.

If we take the "just" to mean "about one day," then we will have a day's waste. We can go on to even smaller time increments, such as an hour, minute, or second, and in all of these cases we are managing the factory based on a waste measure.

The JIT production system uses the "just" in Just-In-Time as a waste gauge. In this sense, this Just concept lies at the very heart of the JIT production system, and this system will not work at factories that have forgotten to eradicate waste as thoroughly as possible. Likewise, a person who doubts the need to thoroughly eliminate waste will not be able to capably carry out JIT improvements.

If the reader is such a person, I suggest he or she put down this manual, and just get back to work.

Lesson 2. Take "Just" to the Max!

Production Is Music: Help Your Factory Play a Masterpiece

I'm not really talking about inviting an orchestra into the factory to perform. But music does serve as an apt metaphor for the sweet harmony of a level-running factory. Production is a lot like music. Waste-free production is like a stirring composition, a masterpiece if you will. Music includes three essential ingredients: melody, rhythm, and harmony. In masterpieces, all three of these elements are masterfully composed and performed. Conversely, no matter how original and alluring the harmony is, if the melody is awkward or the rhythm inconsistent, the result will be less than a masterpiece.

The exact same thing goes for the hum of product-building in factories. What does the factory offer as the closest analogy for melody? On a sheet of music, the melody is usually a string of notes placed according to tone on the five-line treble clef form. I suppose the factory analogy for the melody would be the flow of workpieces from one process to the next. Sometimes this flow continues in straight lines, and at other times it makes U-turns. Sometimes the workpieces move along one at a time, and at other times they flow together in lots.

The most melodic of factory melodies is the "flow manufacturing" system.

What would serve as an analogy for rhythm? There are so many types of rhythm, from the graceful waltz to the snappy tango and the fast-paced rock 'n' roll beat. In the factory, the rhythm is the pitch of production, the rate at which work-in-process moves through the flow of production. We also call this the cycle time. Some products can bebop through the line with a very rapid rhythm while others need to waltz along.

The rhythm of the factory must be "leveled" to keep in pace with the cycle time.

Finally, what can we call the harmony of the factory? Harmony means a concordant combination of tones, a blend that is pleasing to the ear. The factory makes harmony when its people, materials, and machines come together in a waste-free combination that unites all three in harmonic activity.

"Standard operations" are what we use to build such an efficient and harmonious combination of people, materials, and machines.

Thus, production—like music—has three essential ingredients. Flow manufacturing, leveling, and standardized operations are to production what melody, rhythm, and harmony are to music. (See Figure 2.6.)

These three elements make up the lion's share of what is needed to establish JIT production and are the mainstay for introducing the JIT production system. Please remember this as part of the procedure for introducing JIT production. And please remember that it takes much time and effort to create a factory that can delight us with masterpiece production.

Music	=	Production
Melody	=	Flow production (one-piece flow)
Rhythm	=	Leveling (cycle time)
Harmony	=	Standard operations (combination charts and operations charts)

Figure 2.6   The Three Essential Elements of Music and Production.

Lesson 3. Production Is Music

The Next Process Is Your Customer

In Japan, it is not hard to find factories that have "The Next Process Is Your Customer" signs posted here and there. Usually, this saying is understood as referring to the need to provide good quality and to prevent defects. In other words, since the next process is your customer, be sure to deliver only the best products.

However, if you have a close look at these factories, you will find that many of them operate completely under a "push" method of production. This robs some of the true meaning from "The Next Process Is Your Customer" slogan.

When looked at in terms of how goods are moved through the line, there are only two types of production methods. (See Figure 2.7.)

The first is the method in which workpieces that have been finished at one process are immediately sent on to the next process. This is what we call "push" production. Sometimes this method calls for transfer tags to be attached to each workpiece, and the tag is marked each time the workpiece is transferred downstream. In this method, the movement

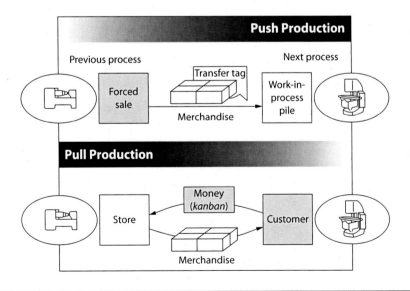

Figure 2.7   Push Production and Pull Production.

of goods is not sensitive to the readiness of the receiving process. At each process, workers simply follow the production schedule in deciding what to do next. Once that is done, they send the finished workpiece along to the next process. We could say that the previous process is "forcing" the sale of its product to the customer at the next process. If the next process does not happen to be ready for the workpiece, the worker there has to say something like, "Oh, you've finished another one already. Well, just set it down over there." Soon there is a work-in-process pile.

In stark contrast to this is the "pull" production method, in which the "customer" at the downstream process goes to the previous process to get "just what is needed, just when it is needed, and in just the amount needed," which he pays for with a currency called *kanban*.

This makes the previous process a sort of "store" that the customer (next process) visits. Of course, the store is responsible for selling only high-quality merchandise to its customers.

The key difference between these two production methods is their respective proximity to the production method called for by the production schedule. In other words, it is the way they relate to the flow between information and materials.

This flow between information and materials is illustrated in Figure 2.8. In the "push" production example, the final assembly schedule (i.e., production schedule) is used as the basis for creating delivery schedules for all of the subassembly, processing, and materials processing stations. All of these stations are part of the in-house production system.

The same delivery schedule also includes delivery deadlines for parts procured from outside vendors and subcontractors. There are various names for this kind of production planning, such as "required volume planning," "parts development," or Material Requirements Planning (MRP). Note that MRP is usually a computer-based system for schedule parts and materials deliveries based on the production schedule.

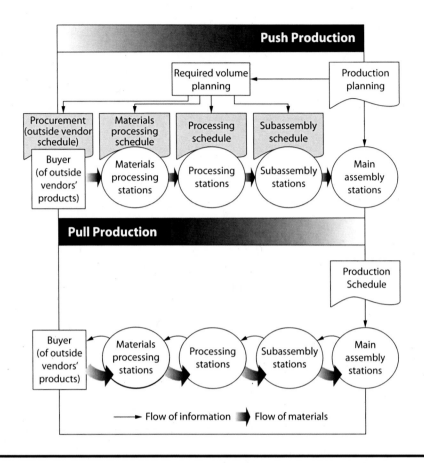

Figure 2.8 Flow of Information and Materials in Push and Pull Production Systems.

Usually, the production schedule must deal with a complex array of components numbering in the hundreds, thousands, or even tens of thousands, and often a computer is brought in to assist in the scheduling tasks.

The major drawback is that the information and materials are not matched. The information is out anywhere between three days and a week before the goods. In other words, the required volume planning is completed several days before the planned products are manufactured at the factory. It is during these several days that the required goods are delivered to the factory and operator instructions are issued.

Another problem is that each process operates according to its own instructions, completely independent of other processes. We call this type of production "independent process production."

Independent process production suffers from inflexibility in the face of scheduling changes. For various reasons, the production schedule might undergo one revision after another, but these changes cannot be easily carried over to the individual production processes. As a result, the first "official" delivery deadlines in the original production schedule become firmly established as each independent process's delivery deadline and are thereafter very difficult to change. The process station's workers tend to regard such last-minute changes as an intrusion and a hassle. This does not bode well for these Japanese factories in today's era of a high yen, ongoing trade friction, and diversifying customer needs.

By contrast, the "pull" production method has, in principle, no delivery schedule save for the final assembly schedule (production schedule). The main assembly processes "pull" just what they need from the subassembly processes. Since the subassembly processes use processed parts, they in turn pull just what they need from the processing line. In other words, nothing happens upstream until something has happened downstream. Since production at the previous (upstream) processes depends on production at the next (downstream) processes, we call this production method "previous process-dependent production." This type of production emphasizes the true importance of the next process as the customer.

In light of these two very different types of production, we could argue that at most of the factories that display "The Next Process Is Your Customer" signs, the real meaning of the signs is "We pretend to use *kanban.*" Unless the factory is actually using pull production instead of push production, its *kanban* do not amount to anything more than a "theoretical" or "decorative" improvement. Unless the factory realizes the importance of matching information with the materials and aggressively revamps its whole production system with a "proactive improvement" attitude, the waste inherent in the push production system will not be removable.

Lesson 4. The Ocean Pulls the Flowing River

"Stop and Go" Production and "Process and Go" Production

A factory where the company president is cautiously watching over the machines and equipment is a tragedy. The main character in this tragedy is not the president, but rather the equipment operators who live under the president's gaze.

Imagine a factory where the company president has just had the latest, most sophisticated equipment brought in, and now stands there telling the operators, "It's your job to operate these things. Get to it!"

Imagine, in this age of diverse models and small lots, a company president having installed all sorts of machines designed for mass production and then commanding the workers, "Set the machines up for the whole range of product models and start turning out products!" Imagine the kind of agony those workers are going through in trying to use machines that are fundamentally incompatible with the factory's needs.

No doubt the company president had thought that the latest machines and equipment would readily solve his factory's various problems.

He may be proud to inform us, "This is great! This new equipment will double our production capacity!" or, "This brand new equipment will take care of our quality problems.

He might even go so far as to claim, "This new equipment will enable us to meet our client's delivery deadlines."

Let us suppose that the factory has usually been incapable of meeting its client's short delivery deadlines, and that is one big reason why the president bought the latest equipment, which is supposed to cut processing time in half. The goal here is to shorten the manufacturing lead-time.

Shortening lead-time by reducing processing time is a mighty bold and eccentric way of doing things. We can spend a fortune on faster processing machines and still not shorten the lead-time one bit. We might succeed, however, in shortening the life of the company.

When we look at production as a flow of materials, we can recognize four main categories of components in this flow: retention, transfer, processing, and inspection. The first thing this teaches us is that making things requires much more than just processing.

As we go through the manufacturing process, imagine that you are one of the parts that has been delivered to the factory and is about to undergo the entire lead-time of the manufacturing process. To start with, you are warehoused along with the other purchased parts and materials. This falls under the "retention" category. Now, it would be nice if the processing machines could walk over to the parts warehouse, pick out the things they need, and process them, but we have not reached that day yet. So the factory needs to move you and all the other goods from the warehouse to the processing machines, a task that falls under the "transfer" category.

Next, you and the other materials that have just been delivered to the processing machines sit in a pile until the machines finish processing the previous lot of materials. This sometimes takes a long time. At last, the machines start in on the first of your lot of materials. You are the last in that lot and are still waiting. All of this waiting is part of the "retention" category.

Finally, you—the last of the lot—are picked up and, in a few brief seconds, get processed. Those fleeting seconds are in the "processing" category.

After being processed, you are plopped onto a pile of processed units. Then you go through another round of retention, transfer to the next group of process machines, more retention, and processing.

To return to our music analogy, we can say that the four parts of this manufacturing process—retention, processing,

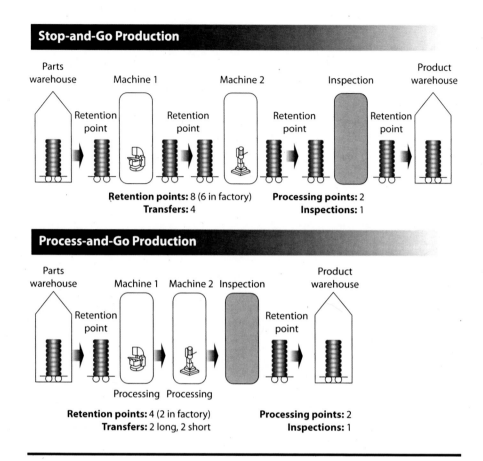

Stop-and-Go Production

Parts warehouse — Machine 1 — Machine 2 — Inspection — Product warehouse

Retention point — Retention point — Retention point — Retention point

Retention points: 8 (6 in factory)
Transfers: 4

Processing points: 2
Inspections: 1

Process-and-Go Production

Parts warehouse — Machine 1 — Machine 2 — Inspection — Product warehouse

Retention point — Retention point

Processing Processing

Retention points: 4 (2 in factory)
Transfers: 2 long, 2 short

Processing points: 2
Inspections: 1

Figure 2.9 **"Stop-and-Go Production" and "Process-and-Go Production."**

retention, and transfer—comprise the four-beat bar of music that most factories use to add value to materials.

Just as only one four-beat bar can hardly be called music, we need to repeat the bar a number of times to create the "music of production." In view of retention's large role in this type of production, we shall call this type "stop-and-go production." (See Figure 2.9).

Within the four-beat, stop-and-go pattern of this type of production, the beats that take up the lion's share of the manufacturing lead-time are the two "retention" beats. In the example shown in Figure 2.9, there are eight retention stages from the parts warehouse to the products warehouse. Six of these retention stages are within the factory, where they directly relate to the manufacturing lead-time.

There are lots of retention points, and together they eat up a lot of time. Once a pile of workpieces is set down somewhere, it tends to stay there for half an hour, an hour, or more. Sometimes part of the pile gets left there overnight to make operations or changeover more convenient. Meanwhile, parts that have been delivered to the parts warehouse can easily wait there for a month or more. Whether the total retention time adds up to hours, days, or weeks, it still eats up a tremendous amount of lead-time. Retention is clearly the worst culprit when it comes to lead-time consumption.

Materials do not do anything but wait at retention points. Having several retention points means we must have some means of moving materials from one retention point to the next. That is where the "transfer" category comes in.

The nice thing about this category is that it never comes close to eating up as much lead-time as the "retention" category can. In most factories, each transfer takes one or two minutes. Still, outside vendors can take several hours to transfer parts and materials to the factory. In any case, out of retention, transfer, and processing, transfer is the second worst culprit.

Inspection is a separate culprit altogether and should be considered apart from the categories that make up the four-beat pattern of production.

Finally, we have the "processing" category, which eats up the least lead-time. A single workpiece's total processing time in the factory commonly adds up to a minute or two. Most individual processes take less than a minute. Some take only several seconds. Press processes usually range between one and two seconds, while drilling machines average about two or three seconds.

It should be obvious by now that bringing in the latest production equipment to shave a few seconds off of the total processing time is not going to help much in reducing the overall lead-time to enable earlier product shipments to customers. A pressing need to meet the client's short delivery deadlines is therefore not much of a reason for any company president to invest in the latest production equipment.

Obviously, the best way to shorten the manufacturing lead-time is to get rid of the worst culprit: retention. Once we do that, our stop-and-go production system can be turned into a "process-and-go" production system in which the four-beat pattern of retention, process, retention, and transfer are replaced by the four-beat pattern of process, transfer, process, and transfer.

Today, shorter lead-times are in big demand by consumers and are also a major factor enabling the expansion of client orders. Old and worn as the expression is, it still rings quite true in the world of manufacturing: "Time Is Money."

> ### *Lesson 5. When the Flow of Goods Stops, the "Lead-Time" Clock Keeps Ticking*

Approach to Efficiency: Estimated Efficiency and True Efficiency

Factories are full of talk about efficiency. Factory people are always trying to improve the equipment operators' efficiency, the equipment's own efficiency, the efficiency of the operations, and various other types of efficiency. The prevalent attitude is, "Let's try to turn out products even just a little bit better than we do now."

Different people, however, have very different understandings of this "efficiency" concept. Most people view such things as efficiency and productivity as a ratio of "output"-to-"input." In other words, people think of productivity as the value of production output divided by the cost of production input. This definition is expressed as an equation below.

$$\text{PRODUCTIVITY} = \frac{\text{PRODUCTION OUTPUT}}{\text{PRODUCTION INPUT}}$$

Assuming that this equation is correct, one could propose three measures for boosting productivity

Measure 1: Increase the production output.

$$\text{PRODUCTIVITY} \uparrow = \frac{\text{PRODUCTION OUTPUT} \uparrow}{\text{PRODUCTION INPUT} \rightarrow}$$

In this equation, I have used arrows to indicate constant levels ($\rightarrow$), increases ($\uparrow$) and decreases ($\downarrow$).

Measure 2: Decrease production input.

$$\text{PRODUCTIVITY} \uparrow = \frac{\text{PRODUCTION OUTPUT} \rightarrow}{\text{PRODUCTION INPUT} \downarrow}$$

Here, we have kept the production output constant ($\rightarrow$) but have lowered ($\downarrow$) the production input, which raises ($\uparrow$) productivity.

Measure 3: Increase production output and decrease production input.

$$\text{PRODUCTIVITY} \uparrow = \frac{\text{PRODUCTION OUTPUT} \uparrow}{\text{PRODUCTION INPUT} \downarrow}$$

This is a combination of Measures 1 and 2, in which we raise ($\uparrow$) productivity by lowering ($\downarrow$) production input and raising ($\uparrow$) production output. Obviously, there are also other ways to boost productivity, and there are various ways of applying the three measures just described.

When we think of "raising" productivity or efficiency, the notion of "raising" tends to lead us first to Measure 1, in which we aim simply to raise production output.

For instance, let us consider the example shown in Figure 2.10. Here, we have a factory that is trying to boost productivity by increasing the number of product units manufactured daily by ten people from 200 units to 250 units.

According to the productivity equations illustrated, the "estimated efficiency" plan in Figure 2.10 should have worked

Figure 2.10 Estimated Efficiency and True Efficiency.

to boost productivity. However, the important thing to note here is that *no matter how much we boost the production output, there is no real gain unless the client's production orders keep pace with the increase.* Making products that are not on order with a client is simply creating waste—overproduction waste and warehouse waste.

The most important equation to remember is:

Volume of orders = Production output

If the current volume of orders and the current production output are both 200 units, there is only one measure to use to boost productivity: Measure 2 (decrease production input). Cutting the required production staff from 10 persons to 8 persons would be a true improvement in efficiency. I would like to stress that *the manpower reduction approach is an indispensable means of improving efficiency.*

Therefore, the JIT production system would have us change the productivity equation to read as follows.

$$\text{VOLUME OF ORDER} = \text{PRODUCTION OUTPUT}$$

$$\text{PRODUCTIVITY} = \frac{\text{PRODUCTION OUTPUT}}{\text{PRODUCTION INPUT}}$$

> ## Lesson 6. The Customer Decides
> ## How to Improve Efficiency

Manpower Reduction

As in the case of "human automation" (*jidoka*) rather than "automation," manpower reduction also has a special meaning within the JIT production system. In Japan, this particular meaning of manpower reduction was born in the 1970s, when oil crises ushered in a "stable growth" era. From about 1955 until the early 1970s, Japan enjoyed a period of rapid economic growth with fast-expanding markets which encouraged manufacturers to restrict the variety of products and maximize the output volumes. Today's commonly known concepts of "automation," "labor reduction," and "manpower reduction" have been inherited from the rapid-growth, small-variety, large-lot era.

The validity of these concepts and their methodologies has steadily diminished in recent years. Market expansion is no longer a given, and consumer needs are clearly becoming more diverse and individualized. In order to continue to provide products attuned to market trends, manufacturers are being forced to switch over to wide-variety, small-lot production.

While expanding product variety and shrinking model-specific volumes, manufacturers must also keep their prices down to succeed in today's highly competitive markets. This difficult business environment encouraged the development of the "worker hour minimization" concept behind JIT's manpower reduction. Basically, this concept says that production should have an output matching market needs, using the minimum number of workers (minimum labor cost) to produce that output in a timely manner. (See Figure 2.11.)

We are all familiar with the popular "labor reduction" and "employee reduction" concepts. Both of these concepts remain within the framework of rigid staff assignment systems. Generally, each equipment operator is responsible for handling only certain different types of equipment. As a

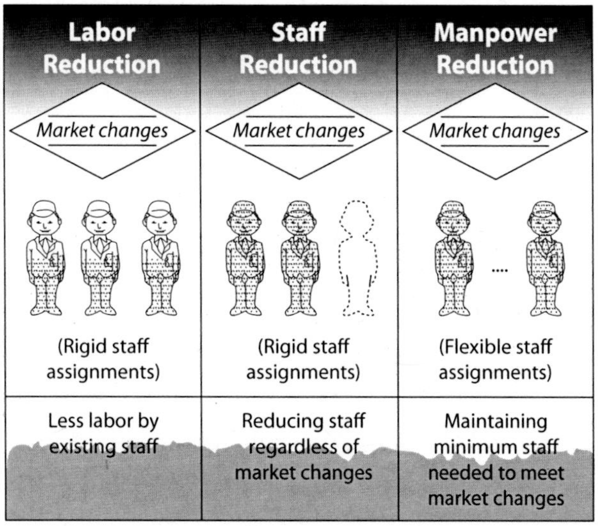

Figure 2.11 Labor Reduction, Staff Reduction, and Manpower Reduction.

result, the staff assignment system is not flexible enough to accommodate suddenly lower market demand for some of the company's products.

Strictly speaking, *labor reduction* means that even when the market demand drops or automation advances, the company does not decrease the number of its workers. Instead, the company only reduces the amount of labor the workers perform. Personnel costs remain the same.

Staff reduction means reducing the number of staff when demand goes down or when automation makes workers redundant. The redundant workers are still kept within the same rigid staff assignment system. This has nothing to do with market fluctuations, but is done simply to reduce staff at certain jobs.

By contrast, *manpower reduction* means promptly changing staff assignments at each process in the factory to reflect the latest market changes. Once it is known what the current client orders are, the factory produces exactly that volume of products while using only the smallest required number of staff. Obviously, this system requires a flexible staff assignment system instead of a rigid system.

Thus, the basic principle of JIT manpower reduction is prompt and flexible adaptation of factory operations and staff assignments to incorporate current market trends. As such, JIT manpower reduction goes hand-in-hand with a flexible production system and contingency management.

The following essential items enable such manpower reduction and market adaptability.

Flow manufacturing—One-piece flow manufacturing in pace with market demands is essential for JIT manpower reduction. Instead of allowing materials and products to pile up, one-piece flow manufacturing turns out just what is needed, just when it is needed, and in just the required amount.

Multi-process handling—This means linking production equipment in lines that suit the flow of products, and having each operator handle several processes within the flow manufacturing system. This requires that operators stand (and walk) while they work, and that they be trained in various equipment-operating skills.

Separating human work and machine work—This process begins by grouping all the little "islands" of operators and their equipment into a flow-oriented line (or manufacturing cell), thus placing together both people and machines. Next, the operators get trained in multi-process handling and are taught how to separate their work from the machine's work. Finally, they work out ways to reduce human work (such as in setting up and removing workpieces) by changing conveyor configurations or other means.

Movable machines—No matter how brilliant an improvement plan is, it may end up in the trash can if machines are unable to be moved to positions specified by the plan. Needless to say, such obstacles can put a damper on enthusiasm for improvement. The worst offenders are the machines that have been bolted to the floor, seemingly stuck there for eternity. Since the market is always changing and improvements make progress from day to day, it only makes sense that equipment

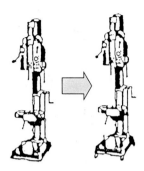

Figure 2.12   Attaching Casters to Make Equipment Movable.

should be movable enough to enable equipment layout changes when switching production over to different product models. Figure 2.12 shows an example of how immovable equipment can be made movable.

Standard operations—Operations that vary from person to person create big problems. Instead, we need to standardize operations and develop *jidoka* to make the operations standard and simple enough for anyone to learn easily. We begin by standardizing current operations and then proceed to make improvements.

Flexible staff assignment system—Instead of the traditional fixed staff assignment system, we should be using a system that is flexible enough to accommodate staff assignment changes in accordance with labor requirements set by market demand.

Mutual aid system—Even the best-laid plans for balanced workloads can run into trouble when the production pitch gets too high or when some other problem causes an imbalance in workloads. To prepare for such eventualities, workers should be able to temporarily lend a hand to adjacent upstream or downstream workers. Such "mutual aid systems" are especially helpful during that tricky phase when process improvements are being worked out. As such, the mutual aid system should be considered a prerequisite for improvement programs.

> ## *Lesson 7. Move from Labor Reduction to Worker Hour Minimization*

Individual Efficiency and Overall Efficiency

Imagine a home electronics manufacturing plant, in which 20 or 30 female assembly workers are standing along an assembly line conveyor, busily building TVs or VCRs. Those not familiar with this kind of work find such an arrangement quite amazing. They also wonder exactly what all those assembly workers are doing.

Almost all of the workers on such assembly lines perform work that includes five or six simple screw turns or wire bonds, and they perform this task over and over all day long. (See Figure 2.13.)

In such cases as this, we set a pitch time of 30 or 40 seconds, then the workers work together trying to keep up the pace. To the ordinary observer, it appears that all of the workers are doing just this. However, someone trained in JIT who has a sharp eye for identifying waste would cite this as a prime example of "idle time waste."

The fact is, if you have 30 people working on a line, their actual production pitch will vary significantly from person to

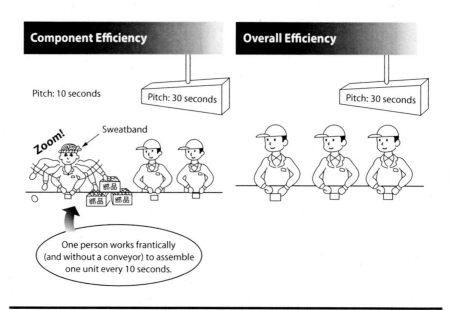

Figure 2.13 Component Efficiency and Overall Efficiency.

person. Some people may always finish in 10 seconds while others struggle and sometimes take longer. Once a worker has finished assembling a unit in 10 seconds, she should have nothing to do but start in on the next unit. This is where conveyors come in handy. They keep the flow moving at one unit per pitch increment. But when a worker finishes early, she must wait out the remainder of that pitch increment until the conveyor brings the next unit. There is nothing she can do for her neighboring workers during this time.

Although everyone claims to be working precisely at the pitch time, faster workers have their work slowed down by slower workers. This kind of "coordinated work" is actually quite susceptible to "idle time waste."

The conveyor's disadvantage is that it tends to hide idle time waste and its advantage is that it keeps things moving at the pitch time. This means that no matter how much improved an individual's efficiency becomes, that improvement can still do nothing to raise the line's overall efficiency. Obviously, it would be quite valuable to have individual efficiency improvements reflected in the line's overall efficiency. But we can see that there is a clear difference between individual efficiency and overall efficiency.

If we take the same assembly line, remove the electric conveyor, and instead have the assembly workers lined up beside one long workbench, the units will gradually begin to pile up next to certain workers due to individual differences in pitch. The piles of work-in-process reveal all those hidden individual differences in pitch.

If we break up the long workbench into individual workbenches for each worker, then the piles of work-in-process become even more obvious.

If we separate the individual workbenches by some distance, it would leave room for work-in-process to pile up indefinitely. The line would soon lose all signs of having a production flow. So you can see why JIT professionals have so little interest in the "coordinated work" arrangement.

This example also underscores the fact that efficiency improvement has nothing to do with upstream or downstream processes and has everything to do with raising efficiency at individual processes. To do this, sometimes factories "automate" a task that is being performed either manually or by a simple machine by installing a high-speed machine, computer-controlled machine, or other absurdly expensive machine.

I sympathize with such factories, and there are a lot of them. In fact, I would say that the vast majority of the world's factories are guilty of these kinds of mistakes.

I am not denying that individual improvements in efficiency can add up to an overall improvement throughout the company. But the improvements have to start with individual people, machines, and processes, and only then should they be developed into improvements in line efficiency, factory-wide efficiency, and company-wide efficiency, including the sales and distribution arms. It is very important to maintain this kind of comprehensive view of efficiency improvement.

Once management installs and activates highly sophisticated and ultra-expensive machinery on the production line to improve efficiency at certain processes, it is naturally concerned about getting its money's worth. This leads it to press for higher and higher capacity utilization rates. In the meantime, the idea of letting client orders determine production output gets put on the back burner.

In this day and age, the comfortable notion that if a product is made, it will sell one way or another, no longer holds true. The smart idea for today is, "Let's make only what will sell, but make it more efficiently." Once we take this perspective, pushing up capacity utilization for its own sake is clearly a mistake.

Pressing and forging processes are prime targets for managers who limit their view to process-specific efficiency improvements. Both of these processes require die changeover, which tends to take a long time. The managers try to minimize this time consumption by minimizing the number of necessary die changes. The way to do that is by making fewer models in larger lots. Soon the factory is back to the old large-lot orientation. The problem is the managers' belief that the fewer the die changes, the higher the efficiency.

These managers have forgotten that production includes more than pressing and forging processes. *Unless production is made level throughout all processes, the overall result may well be a loss in efficiency.*

The JIT production system not only includes techniques for thoroughly eliminating waste, it also includes techniques for creating and maintaining a level production flow. We need to stand firmly behind both of these principles.

> ## Lesson 8. Where Muddy Streams Appear, Floods May Follow

Approach to Waste: Just-In-Time and Cost Reduction

"We've found it! Now let's get rid of it!" Words such as these are often used by improvement teams that finally pinpoint a true cause of waste, inconsistency, or irrationality and set about making the improvement to eliminate it.

The Just-In-Time concept is a very effective tool for eliminating these three evils. It is especially useful for eradicating waste in such common manifestations as "overproduction waste," "idle time waste," "conveyance waste," and "warehouse waste."

Figure 2.14 illustrates some of the essential ingredients in any well-organized effort to eliminate waste and cut costs.

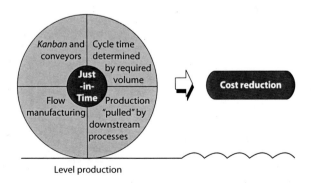

Figure 2.14   Just-In-Time and Cost Reduction.

These ingredients are described below.

1. *Cycle time is determined by the required amount*

   Usually, factory managers use equipment capacity and/or manpower resources as a basis for determining the cycle time or pitch. That is a big mistake. If, for instance, we know that our equipment can handle a 20-second pitch, but our client orders are not enough to cover the resulting amount of production volume, we are going to have a product glut. Conversely, if we select a pitch that is too slow to keep up with client orders, we will have a product shortage.

   Obviously, the right thing to do is make client orders the basis for setting the cycle time or pitch.

2. *Production is "pulled" by downstream processes*

   Unlike the flow of rivers, the impetus for the production flow should not be upstream processes "pushing" the work-in-process to downstream processes, but rather downstream processes "pulling" the work-in-process from upstream processes. In other words, the worker at the next process is truly the customer in that he or she goes to the "store" (the previous process) and "buys" what is needed. This effectively prevents unneeded work-in-process from being passed downstream.

3. *Implement flow manufacturing*

   Just-In-Time production is impossible as long as work-in-process is grouped into lots, which we call "shish-kabob" production. Instead, work-in-process must move in single units all along the "flow manufacturing" line.

4. *Use* kanban *and conveyors between appropriate processes*

   Flow manufacturing stands at the very core of Just-In-Time production and is therefore essential to the JIT production system. However, the current level of technology for certain processes that involve heat treatment or gilding still require the lot production method (or subcontracting). It is therefore appropriate to use *kanban* and conveyors between these processes.

5. *Level production is a prerequisite*

In order to make all of the factory's processes flow as level as possible, we need to have a thoroughly even distribution of product models and volumes. Once we have leveled the assembly lines, we can synchronize them and level them with the subassembly lines, and finally the parts processing lines.

Lesson 9. The Amount of Cost Reduction Achieved Is Proportionate to the Amount of Effort Invested

---

When Economical Lot Sizes Are Not Economical

As mentioned earlier, pressing and forging processes require metal dies. Drilling processes need bits, and cutting processes need blades. As for the assembly processes, they need to deal with multiple components. None of these facts pose any problems as long as the factory produces only one product model. But single-product factories are an endangered species.

In today's manufacturing world, factories must always be switching their production from one product model to the next. Naturally, this means that metal dies must be changed at pressing and forging processes. Drill bits and blades need to be changed at drilling and cutting processes. And component sets need to be changed at assembly processes. We use the term "changeover" in reference to all of these types of equipment set-up work.

Not surprisingly, workers tend to dislike changeover and would much prefer to avoid product model changes by sticking with single-model large-lot production. Large lots are naturally more popular at factories than small ones. But anyone responsible for managing the company's operating capital will be quick to point out that there must be limits to

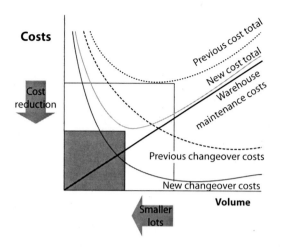

Figure 2.15   Changeover Improvement for Smaller Lots and Lower Costs.

lot sizes. The need to balance these opposite interests gave rise to the "economical lot sizes" concept.

As shown in Figure 2.15, the economical lot size is the lot size that achieves the best balance between (that is, the lowest total for) inventory maintenance costs and changeover costs.

It is not too difficult to understand how economical lot sizes can be determined based on process-specific cost measures. However, this method of determination may not work so easily on a larger scale, such as an entire production line or an entire factory.

On such larger scales, it becomes apparent that making lot sizes even just a little smaller will benefit such economical considerations as lower warehouse investment costs, turnover of operating assets, profit ratio, and cash flow.

We also need to remember that production lead-time is not simply the sum of process-specific operation times. Lead-time is actually proportionate to production lot size, which is to say the amount of work-in-process. Therefore, a long lead-time means that a great deal of work-in-process must still be manufactured before the product can be shipped. If production schedule changes are made after a production run has already begun, the flow of materials and information in the factory—and the flow of management processes—will all fall into disorder. Production cannot be made that flexible.

In JIT, we use "factory graveyards" as a nickname for the kind of warehouse inventories factories accumulate when they stick to large-lot production. Such factories may seem impressive in the huge array of materials they contain, but their true "insides"—full of concealed waste and other problems—are in pretty bad shape.

Today, factories should not resemble those large, awesome, but hopelessly outdated beasts known as dinosaurs. Rather, they should be more like small, agile, and alert mice.

Once we have managed to shorten the manufacturing lead-time, we can responsibly shorten the main schedules, such as for sales and production, and can be more flexible toward schedule changes. As a result, we can help minimize "lost opportunities" in marketing.

In dealing with today's fast-paced technological advances, we can also help minimize the impact of all-too-frequent design changes. In other words, having a shorter lead-time is a key factor enabling adaptability to changing sales figures. It also saves time. And since time is money, it saves money.

Thus, smaller lots do not necessarily mean higher costs.

When we look at the various components of warehouse maintenance costs, we find: *interest, insurance, taxes, storage costs, and obsolescence costs.*

How do these costs compare with higher changeover costs incurred by small-lot production? Such costs include: *manufacturing-related clerical costs, mechanical changeover costs, loss of materials, and set-up and removal (labor) costs.*

Let us take a close look at these two sets of component costs. It should be easy enough to spot which set is most conducive to improvements.

In the first set of component costs, almost all of them resist improvement, no matter how hard the company employees might try to attack them. For instance, the only way to reduce warehouse maintenance costs is by decreasing lot sizes.

By contrast, the component costs for changeover—such as the manufacturing-related clerical costs, mechanical changeover costs, and loss of materials—are all amenable to improvement if people get together and brainstorm some improvement ideas. In short, these costs are prime targets for JIT improvement activities.

In fact, JIT shows us how we can even get rid of our fixed idea of "lots" by changing factories into a level system where products are built in short production runs without disturbing the overall flow of the factory.

> ## Lesson 10. Do Not Neglect the Economic Forest by Focusing on Economic Trees

Motion and Work

One of the things factory workers tend to mumble on their way out the gate at the end of the day is something along the lines of, "Man, I worked my tail off today."

Ordinarily, we take such expressions at face value. But if we look beneath the surface, we will find that different people have widely different understandings of the meaning of "work." Some people feel that simply being at the company for eight hours is work. These people make time their measure of work, in that every minute or even every second they spend at the company is regarded as work. They watch the clock and keep careful track of their overtime as defined in the employee's manual.

Other people evaluate work in terms of "sweat." There is a long tradition in Japan and in the West of regarding a person's perspiration as irrefutable evidence that he or she is hard at work. People are suspicious of work that does not cause the worker to sweat. In fact, given a choice between two equally productive work methods—one that produces sweat and one that does not—they will usually pick the sweat-producing method.

Then there are people who derive their sense of work satisfaction from the "added value" their work produces. These are just a few of the different ways people understand the meaning of work.

I would suggest that the people I first described—the "time" workers—are actually more "not working" than working. The "sweat work" people perform more motion than work. It is the "added value" people that come closest of the three to actually working. For simplicity's sake, we will include the "not working" people in with the "moving" people.

As I mentioned earlier, people have different perceptions of work. Even within a single day's work time, we can recognize such differences between the "moving" people and the "working" people.

Equipment operators ordinarily work an eight-hour day. Obviously, not all of that eight-hour time is spent working. In fact, the great majority of that time is spent "moving" rather than "working." (See Figure 2.16.)

As noted in Figure 2.16, "work" is only the part of the operations that actually adds value. Every other part of the

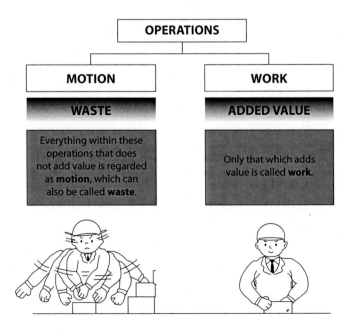

Figure 2.16   Motion and Work.

operations is called "motion" rather than "work." In everyday work operations, there is rarely a clear distinction between actions that actually are "working" and those that merely are "moving." The two just mix together in our overall actions. What seems to be "working" at one instant may turn into "moving" at another, and vice versa.

It is not easy for an untrained eye to distinguish between the two. Many factories make the careless mistake of starting out their improvement campaigns with the general notion that whatever moves is work and what does not is waste. Obviously, their improvement campaigns are not going to be very successful until they learn to make the distinction between "work" and "motion."

Waste that is not recognizable as such is the most insidious kind of waste. If we can learn to recognize this kind of waste, we are well on our way to success in eradicating waste.

The following is a list of some of the things we might encounter as we stroll through a typical factory. Odds are that we would not be able to recognize these motions as 10 examples of waste.

1. Workers grunting and groaning as they carry a heavy load.
2. Workers counting parts once the operation is done.
3. Workers moving stacks of parts from the floor to a cart.
4. Workers inserting parts into plastic bags before sending them downstream.
5. Workers removing the plastic bags from parts received.
6. Workers who have finished today's work and are proudly starting in early on tomorrow's.
7. Workers securing parts to be processed.
8. Workers repeating the cycle of picking up parts, processing them, and setting them down elsewhere.
9. Workers watching out for defects while their machines are operating.
10. Workers searching for parts, tools, or jigs.

The above are 10 typical examples of waste in factories. I could list more. In fact, I could fill this entire book with typical examples of waste. That is how much waste exists in factories.

Imagine standing with the president of the company that owns the factory and watching such a waste-filled factory in operation. What do you suppose the president might say if you remarked, "Boy, your workers are really moving around a lot, aren't they?"

Unfortunately, a large number of company presidents would respond with something like, "Yeah, our factory people really work hard for us."

Personally, I would not blame you if you responded to that by making a sour bulldog face and stomping out of the factory. When people fail to recognize the difference between "motion" and "work," you can be sure their eyes are blind to waste. Let us see just how different "motion" and "work" really are.

The only result of motion is higher costs. Well, actually, it has one other result: eating up profits. Now you see why we call "motion" waste. In sharp contrast to this, the result of "work" is to fulfill a function. This function is generally a value-adding function.

Motion and work are mixed together within the typical equipment operator's activities. But motion (waste) is clearly the main ingredient. As a result, the equipment operator's activities actually add very little value.

Consider the example of a press operator illustrated in Figure 2.17.

1. *The first step in the press operator's activity: picking up and moving an unprocessed workpiece.*
   This movement adds absolutely no value to the workpiece. Therefore, it is an example of waste. The waste can be reduced by shortening the distance of this movement. Of course, the best thing would be to eliminate the movement (and the waste) altogether.

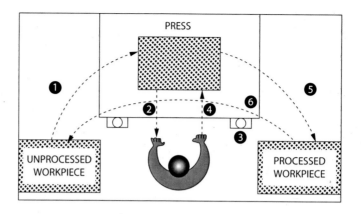

Figure 2.17   Activity of a Press Operator.

2. *The second step: moving a hand to push a button.*

   A complete waste. The worker's hand is not holding anything and is moving through empty air.

3. *The third step: pushing the button.*

   During the instant it takes to push the button, the worker is adding value to the workpiece. To be precise, this button-pushing operation takes about one second, assuming the press is a relatively small one weighing about 100 tons. And while we are being precise, we should note that even that one-second button-pushing operation includes some waste. The time it takes the upper die to reach the workpiece—the time the upper die spends pressing nothing but air—is waste. And that accounts for almost all of the time it takes to press the workpiece. And we should also note that in this process, it is the machine—not the worker—that adds the value.

4. *The fourth step: moving a hand to remove the workpiece.*

   Again, the worker moves his hand through empty air. All waste.

5. *The fifth step: removing the processed workpiece, moving it, and setting it down nearby.*

   Moving the workpiece is just handling time. All waste.

6. *The sixth step: moving to pickup the next unprocessed workpiece.*

   All motion, no work. All waste.

In this example, the easiest way to reduce waste is to reduce the distance the worker must move in order to pickup unprocessed workpieces and set down processed ones.

As just described, almost everything that happened in this example was a form of waste. We should remember that anytime "working" means taking workpieces down from shelves, setting them down, or carrying them somewhere, it is not actually "work," but "motion." And *motion means waste.*

Recently, companies have started to rationalize their conveyance and improve their material handling procedures, in many cases by introducing Automated Guided Vehicles (AGVs) or other automatic material handling vehicles. These devices are generally very well received in factories, since they spare workers the chore of having to lug materials around. But they should not be viewed so optimistically.

Generally, these automatic transport systems do little or nothing to speed up material handling or shorten the distance involved therein. The best approach is to think, "Let's cut off transport-related waste at the root."

I call this kind of automation "skin-deep automation" or "make-believe automation," since in the final analysis it just creates conveyance-related, equipment-related, and energy-related waste. The genuine solution is to begin by organizing and regulating the factory to improve the equipment layout to the point where they no longer need conveyors of any kind. The idea is to proceed with caution before adopting any simple "automation" plan.

> ## Lesson 11. Operations Should Flow Like a Clear Stream

Inherited Waste and Inherent Waste

No matter how good a factory is at manufacturing products, you can bet that it stands knee-deep in waste. Starting with the most obvious, we could cite a typical factory for having too wide a "green belt" around it, having too large a building, having management functions that no one seems to understand, and so on.

Waste can be found hiding in even the most magnificent factories. And in factories at the other end of the quality spectrum, just about everything we see is waste.

I remember when, during one factory inspection tour, the company president first led me into what appeared to be a warehouse. Everywhere I looked I saw parts, products, and boxes stacked almost to the ceiling. I advised that we look at the factory and then come back to the warehouse. Then the company president's smile dropped into a frown as he said, "This *is* the factory."

In an attempt to lessen his embarrassment, I offered, "Oh, I thought it was a warehouse since there aren't any workers here."

But my host's face only turned a brighter shade of red. "No, they're over there, behind those boxes," he said.

He was right. There they were, hidden from view by stacks of boxes, as if playing hide-and-seek.

The situation was so bad in that factory that I saw a worker stretching to place more parts boxes on top of a stack that was already too high. Like a stack of pennies, the stack reached the point of instability and I began to wonder if it would fall.

Just as I saw the stack swaying dangerously to one side, another worker appeared out of nowhere just in time to help set the stack even. The company president and I applauded their fast-thinking teamwork.

Then I thought to myself, "It's amazing that such a spirit of cooperation survives in a place like this!"

This whole affair makes for a humorous anecdote, but there is nothing funny about it as far as the company's future is concerned. In fact, there are a great number of factories that are just as comical and just as pitiful. It is no exaggeration to say that, in most cases, it is not a matter of finding waste in the factory, but of finding the factory in the waste.

These days, I often hear of factories that, barely turning a profit, suddenly decide to "rationalize" and "modernize" by installing computer-based management and robot systems. Meanwhile, waste lives on as a nonendangered species. The waste lives on in new forms as the factory is reorganized, computerized, and automated. JIT improvement experts call this "systematic waste-making" and regard it with unmitigated disgust.

Let us take an example of "waste-making computerization."

Once a factory introduces a new production system, the managers need to make up a new bill of materials. Such bills of materials are used to indicate which parts are needed to build which products. (See Figure 2.18.)

The various steps (or "layers") in the production system from the materials stage to the final product stage is called the "depth" of the bill of materials. Generally, more complex products have deeper bills of materials.

Consequently, some manufacturers are proud of having very deep bills of materials, since this is seen as evidence of how complex and sophisticated their products are. In most cases, though, the depth of a bill of materials is much more a function of how complicated the production system is than a function of product complexity.

The reason why a part or assembly part gets established as an item in the bill of materials is that the part requires some kind of "management." Generally, these kinds of items include:

- Materials: ordering and delivery management (*order management*).
- Parts (group 1): work instructions (*operation management*).
- Parts (group 2): work-in-process planning (*work-in-process management*).
- Parts (group 3): supplies for outside vendors (*supplies management*).
- Assembly parts: feed assembly parts to assembly lines (*assembly feed management*).

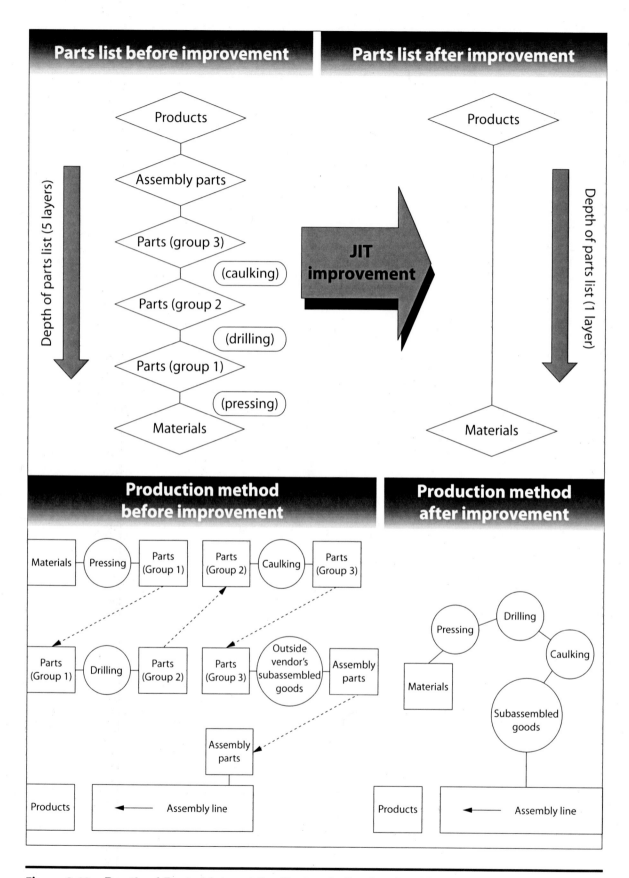

Figure 2.18 **Depth of Parts List and the Factory's Production Method.**

In the factory, where work-in-process stocks tend to pile up, work-in-process management, as well as operation management aimed at preventing defects and improving efficiency, are important enough to warrant inclusion as items in the bill of materials.

However, we should also regard including these items in the bill of materials as evidence that work-in-process tends to pile up and that the flow of goods does not always flow in a level manner. Perhaps the work-in-process piles up precisely because the flow of goods is not level. The piling up of work-in-process creates the need for management. The managers then want to have a computer to help them manage the flow of goods.

Once they bring a computer in, a waste-filled flow of goods gets augmented by a waste-filled flow of information. The end result is a waste-filled production management system.

Naturally, any system that creates so much waste is bound to have a deep bill of materials. And as the bill of materials gets deeper, more and more things get included as items to be handled at the factory. The vast numbers of items to be handled and accounted for create a need for an expensive, sophisticated computer system.

The factory now includes a whole new task: entering the long (and still growing) list of bill of materials items into the computer system. And then there is the additional big task of revising the computerized bill of materials whenever the bill is changed, due to things like the installation of new equipment. A third computer-related task is the lengthy processing required to calculate the required material orders for such a deep bill of materials. All those computer-related tasks create the need for a staff of trained computer programmers and operators. As you can see, waste creates more waste.

The same kind of self-perpetuating growth of waste can occur when factories hastily introduce industrial robots or other automated equipment. A waste-filled factory becomes an automated waste-filled factory. The waste gets processed automatically by systems such as AGVs, automated warehouses, and other automatic material handling lines.

The worst part of this phenomenon is that waste that would have been relatively easy to identify and remove becomes much more firmly embedded and hidden in the manufacturing system after it is carried over into sophisticated systems such as automated production lines. Waste gets harder and harder to remove. Eventually, it gets to the point where the entire factory, or even the entire company, must be torn apart to be improved.

Lesson 12. Remove Waste Before It Sinks Deeper

Improving the Intensity and Density of Labor

Generally, we tend to think of improvements, rationalization, and removing waste as means of intensifying labor. In factories where workers have strong unions, there has sometimes been a great deal of resistance to such changes. Naturally, the changes have to be worked out in negotiations with the union leadership.

Union leaders have sometimes expressed opinions such as: "We're already working as hard as we can! There's just no room for improvement."

Not surprisingly, such narrow-minded thinking usually comes from companies that are operating in the red. Such thinking also shows just how little the employees understand about the waste hidden in work operations.

As explained earlier, each work operation consists of two parts: "motion," which is action that does not directly add value to the workpiece and is therefore waste, and "work" which does add value. Motion—the wasteful part—is usually by far the larger of the two parts.

JIT improvement is a program for thoroughly removing the enormous amount of waste hidden in work operations. Figure 2.19 illustrates the waste elimination technique that forms the basis of JIT improvement.

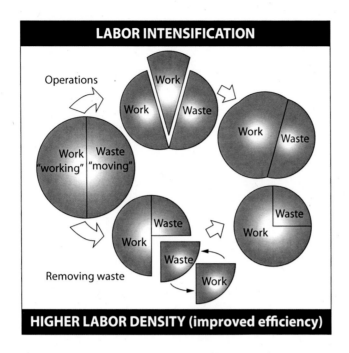

Figure 2.19 Improvement of Labor Intensity and Labor Density.

If we were to simply increase the amount of work without removing waste, the workers would have a very good reason to complain. Such a change would be nothing more than intensifying their labor.

We need to make a large and important distinction between the *intensity* and the *density* of labor. Intensifying labor without removing waste aims solely to increase production output. For instance, we can require the workers to work faster, which would raise the production output. This is what intensified labor alone means.

This is *not* the right way to go about improving things. We need to take a very different approach—improving labor density. We start by finding and removing waste from within work processes. More specifically, this waste elimination stage includes:

- Understanding the entire work process.
- Quickly recognizing the actual value-adding function of the process.

- Applying the concepts of "motion" and "work" to study the work process.
- Distinguishing clearly between wasteful "motion" and value-adding "work."
- Immediately doing whatever is possible to remove wasteful "motion" from the work process.

Let us consider an example. A certain press worker's work process starts with fetching a workpiece from a site about eight feet away and pressing it. The first improvement is to have the workpieces set close enough so that the worker does not need to take any steps to reach them. That one improvement removes 16 feet (round trip) of "walking waste" or about six seconds of "time waste."

Now, what shall the worker do with these six seconds of freed-up time? Ideally, they should be used for value-adding actions. If this can be done, we can "naturally" (that is, without strain) translate that much more labor time into higher production output. In other words, we can increase the production output *without intensifying labor.* The worker will work at the same speed as before, but will "naturally" have greater output.

The more we can increase the ratio of "work" to "motion" within a work process, the greater the density of labor becomes. By definition, higher labor density means more value is added to the product per unit of labor cost.

Now you can see why we call removing waste the very basis of JIT improvement. The thing that JIT improvement team members need to be most careful in checking is whether or not their improvements actually remove waste.

In view of the above, it is fair to say that *JIT improvement does not in any way require intensification of labor.*

Any worker in any factory should be able to confirm this for him or herself. If the worker feels that an improvement has sped up the work or has made it more *difficult, it can only be a sign of errors in the improvement.*

> ## Lesson 13. Removing Waste Means Turning Wasteful Motions into Productive Work

Approach to Inventory and Lead-Time: Inventory and Lead-Time

Everyone—the manufacturers and their clients—face a highly competitive business environment. In the economic jungle—as in the real jungle—you either eat or are eaten. This harsh business environment has led to rising client demands for lower costs and shorter delivery deadlines. For their part, factories seek "compressed delivery deadlines."

Imagine some company managers who, faced with tough market competition, come to you for advice on how to shorten delivery deadline periods by as much as 50 percent. Let us also assume that the factory managers have already tried installing new equipment and implementing a TQC program, but without the expected results. They are getting desperate for answers.

Now imagine how surprised they would be if you were to simply suggest, "That's easy enough, just reduce your current inventory 50 percent." No doubt, they would probably appear mystified and wonder how the subject of conversation got switched from delivery deadlines to inventory. Again, you need only explain, "What's the mystery? It's really very simple. Just cut the current production lot sizes in half."

Now watch what happens. Their minds, already bewildered by your connection of delivery deadlines and less inventory, collapse into total confusion as they consider yet a third apparently unrelated factor: lot size.

Maybe someone will seek to clarify things by asking, "Let me get this straight. We cut delivery deadlines in half by cutting inventory in half, which means cutting lot sizes in half. But doesn't that mean we'll also be cutting our production output in half?"

Now they are getting somewhere. You can continue by adding, "Cut output in half? Yes, I suppose it does. But you can fix that by doubling the number of production runs." Again, mass confusion. "Wait a minute. We cut inventory and lots in half and then we double the production run?"

By now, their brains' logic circuits have probably shorted out and their ears are about ready to start spurting fireworks. That might be a good point to end the consulting session, and just leave them to think about it.

It is truly amazing how many top managers at manufacturing companies are ignorant of basic production principles. They should at least be able to immediately recognize the relationship between lead-time and inventory.

Let us look at the line chart shown in Figure 2.20 below.

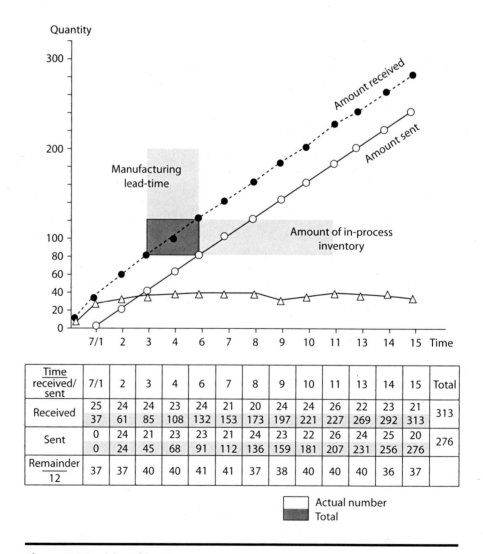

Time received/ sent	7/1	2	3	4	6	7	8	9	10	11	13	14	15	Total
Received	25	24	24	23	24	21	20	24	24	26	22	23	21	313
	37	61	85	108	132	153	173	197	221	227	269	292	313	
Sent	0	24	21	23	23	21	24	23	22	26	24	25	20	276
	0	24	45	68	91	112	136	159	181	207	231	256	276	
Remainder $\overline{12}$	37	37	40	40	41	41	37	38	40	40	40	36	37	

Actual number
Total

Figure 2.20 Line Chart.

The vertical axis in this chart represents "quantity" while the horizontal axis stands for "time." The broken line shows the "amount received" and the solid line the "amount sent." Manufacturing lead-time is what fills any gap between the amount received and the amount sent. Wider gaps mean longer lead-times. Moreover, longer lead-times mean larger amounts of in-process inventory.

In other words, the relationship between manufacturing lead-time and in-process inventory can be described using the following two equations.

$$\text{Manufacturing lead-time =}$$
$$\text{in-process inventory expressed in day units}$$

$$\text{Amount of in-process inventory =}$$
$$\text{manufacturing lead-time} \times \text{daily production output}$$

Although our example refers to in-process inventory, it can be applied similarly to inventories of products or materials. If we cut our product inventory in half, we need to cut our lead-time in half, too. The same goes for our material inventory. If we cut that in half, we need to cut the delivered lots in half and double the number of deliveries.

In the factory, problems crop up in all kind of areas, including delivery deadlines, quality, and inventories. None of these problems exist independently of the others. They are all interrelated, and we must learn how they connect.

Factories having trouble meeting delivery deadlines are probably also suffering from excess inventory, difficulty in switching to wide-variety and small lots, and ongoing missing parts and other defects. All of this relates to what we call "the character of the factory." The most visible aspect of this "character" is inventory. The inventory situation is so visible that a JIT consultant can generally appraise it immediately upon entering the factory.

Inventory is the JIT consultant's best teacher.

Lesson 14. Inventory Tells the Whole Story

Why Is Inventory Bad?

Many of us think of inventory as a "necessary evil."

During times of booming markets and brisk sales, we appreciate the necessity of inventory as the "ammunition" for doing business. But when the market boom fizzles out and sales slump, we suddenly feel the "evil" of inventory, too. Inventory is thus a two-faced entity, sometimes an angel and sometimes a devil. In JIT production, inventory always has only one face: the Devil's.

If you were to ask me why inventory is a bad thing, I could give you the following general reasons.

1. *Inventory adds weight to the interest payment burden*
   Anytime we need to procure capital, we must pay the cost of such capital. The general term for this cost is "interest." For whatever amount of time the materials purchased with such capital sit "idle" as inventory, the invested capital does nothing except incur interest debt and is therefore a pure and simple addition to the company's interest payment burden.

2. *Inventory takes up space*
   Obviously, inventory has some bulk and therefore needs space. If we allow inventory to accumulate, we soon must either put up with cramped factory floors or must invest further capital in new shelves or new warehouse facilities.

3. *Inventory creates the need to convey and handle waste*
   Stopping something to keep it in one place implies movement before and after the stopping. Moving things to intermediate locations from where they will need to be moved again, and loading and unloading these things from the conveyors are all forms of waste.

4. *Inventory invites defects*
   If left idle long enough, "nonperishable" items will begin to rust or otherwise suffer time-related deterioration.

Simple logic also dictates that the more times a thing is handled, the greater its chance of receiving dents or other damage-related defects through mishandling.

5. *Inventory creates unnecessary management costs*

We incur storage costs whenever we stop the flow of goods and we incur transportation management costs whenever we move those goods. The more defects we have, the more we must put out for QC. A poorly-run factory eventually finds itself up to its ears in management costs.

6. *Inventory eats up valuable stocks of materials and parts*

We cannot make products out of thin air. We must have the materials and parts to make them. If we use our current inventory of materials and parts to make products that cannot be sold immediately, and therefore sit idly as product warehouse inventory, we have eaten up stock of materials and parts—the value of which will become painfully clear if a big order comes in for a different product that we now lack the components to make.

7. *Inventory gobbles up costly energy*

Unnecessary inventory means unnecessary consumption of energy. Whether that be electricity, pneumatic or hydraulic power, or whatever, the company has to pay for it.

These are just some of the "evils" of inventory. And I have not even mentioned the real reason why inventory is bad. When you get right down to it, *inventory is bad because it conceals the factory's problems.*

All factories have problems. Problems pile up in even the very best factories. Inventory casts a sort of camouflaging shroud over these problems, and this makes the problems that much harder to analyze and solve.

For instance, workers at a process that turns out defective products by the dozens may choose to pile up a "buffer" stock of products for inspection. The inspectors can identify and

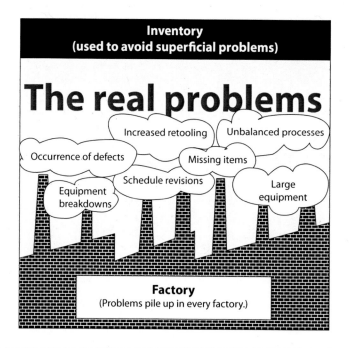

Figure 2.21   How Inventory Conceals Problems in the Factory.

pull out the defective products and thereby prevent "passing along trouble" to the next process. But this solution only covers up the real problem, which is the process's tendency to turn out defective goods. The inspection stock (inventory) solves the superficial problem of "passing along trouble" but does nothing to address the real problem. (See Figure 2.21.)

The more a factory uses inventory to escape its peripheral problems and avoid dealing with its real problems, the more the real problems will grow, sending roots deeper and deeper into the manufacturing system. Eventually, they begin to weaken the very "character" of the factory. In this way, it is fair to call inventory "the opium of the factory." Like an opium habit, the inventory habit is best never started.

Lesson 15. Inventory Is the Opium of the Factory

Inventory and Finance

Just about everything under the sun has some sort of function. One gizmo's function is to take in coins and dole out refreshments, while another's is to conduct electricity and convert it into light. Everything that has a function requires some kind of input and produces some kind of output. In many cases, that output becomes some other thing's input.

The same principle can be seen at work in companies. In the case of manufacturing companies, they acquire capital, lay in stocks of materials, turn these materials into products, and then sell the products to acquire, among other things, recyclable capital.

We find a similar situation when we switch from managing materials to managing money—which many regard as the pivotal aspect of company management. Put very briefly, the function of finance management is to procure and operate capital. Capital procurement is the input and capital operation is the output.

Now we are ready to ask, "What is inventory's role within the context of this money-recycling activity we call finance management?"

Please look at the balance sheet shown in Figure 2.22. The right side of the balance sheet is the credit side, which lists liabilities and shareholders' equity. The left side is the assets side. Usually, the capital procurement figures are listed in the liabilities section while the operating figures are listed in the assets section.

In the balance sheet shown in the figure, the assets and liabilities are listed in ascending order of "fluidity." To make this fluidity a little easier to grasp, we added a downward arrow and the term "cash-convertible" next to the credit side. This cash-convertible arrow indicates that the lower an item is positioned on the assets list, the easier that item is to convert into cash.

As we can see in the balance sheet, inventory items such as finished goods, work-in-process, and materials are positioned within the more cash-convertible category of "current assets." However, they are not as cash-convertible as other items in that category, such as cash, notes receivable, and

Balance Sheet Summary (As of [date])		
Assets	**Liabilities**	
I. Current Assets	I. Current Liabilities	
Cash x x	Notes payable x x	
Notes receivable x x	Accounts payable—trade x x	
Accounts receivable—trade x x	Short-term loans payable x x	
Finished goods x x	Accrued amount payable x x	
Work-in-process x x	and accrued expense	
Materials x x	Allowance for taxes x x	
II. Fixed Assets	II. Fixed Liabilities	
Property, plant, equipment	Bonds payable x x	
Buildings x x	Long-term loans payable x x	
Machinery and equipment x x	Allowance for employee x x	
Land x x	retirement benefits	
Intangible fixed assets	Total Liabilities x x x	
Good will x x	**Shareholders' Equity**	
Patent rights x x		
Investment and other assets	I. Capital stock x x	
Investments in securities x x	II. Legal Reserve of x x	
Investments x x	Retained Earnings	
III. Deferred Charges x x	III. Surplus	
	Voluntary reserves x x	
	Unappropriated retained x x	
	earnings at end of term	
	(Earnings at end of term) x(x x)	
	Total shareholder's equity) x x x	
Total Assets x x x	**Total Liabilities and Shareholders' Equity** x x x	

Left margin: Operation / Cash-convertible
Right margin: Procurement / Reimbursable

Figure 2.22   Position of Inventory in a Corporate Balance Sheet.

trade-related accounts receivable. In fact, they are the least cash-convertible of all of the current assets.

The task of managing a company's activities begins with procuring capital. If this procured capital can be recycled within a year, it is considered a "current liability." If recycling takes a year or more, it becomes a "fixed liability." In either case, having use of the capital incurs a capital cost known as interest.

As mentioned earlier, the company uses this interest-bearing capital to lay in stocks of parts and other materials, add value to the materials through manufacturing, then sell the finished goods for a profit, part of which can be recycled into further capital.

The gist of the problem is that people in these companies work so hard to earn the profit used to recycle capital, only to waste that capital by "putting it to sleep" in raw materials, work-in-process (in which some value has already been added), and products that do not "move" but just sit there as inventory.

Capital costs "move" with the clock and thus never sleep. The company must keep paying these costs while its inventory snores away.

It should be apparent by now just how much inventory betrays the whole principle of finance, which is to "procure and operate capital." Although businesspeople make use of the term "inventory investment," the truth is that inventory alone offers no return on investment and therefore should not be considered an investment at all. How helpful it would be if everyone kept this simple fact in mind.

Lesson 16. Inventory Is Not an Investment

When "Appropriate" Inventory Is Not Appropriate

People in training for the job of inventory management often run into texts with titles along the lines of, "Inventory: Not Too Much and Not Too Little Keeps Production Running Smoothly." "Not Too Much" foreshadows the text's admonitions to drastically reduce inventory.

But what does "Not Too Little" refer to? It refers to a common piece of advice: Make sure you have at least some excess inventory. It does not mean "minimize" inventory. It says that we are supposed to maintain a little "fat" in the inventory, but not too much.

The philosophy behind this "keep a little fat" approach to inventory is that having a little extra inventory on hand as a sort of "buffer" will enable the factory to respond quickly to surprise sell-outs or shortages of materials and products. However, in view of the wide range of products demanded of factories by today's diversifying market needs, how little can "a little fat" really be and still serve as a buffer? We have to face the fact that, in today's marketplace, surprise sell-outs and parts shortages are still bound to happen when we maintain a slightly (or even seriously) overweight inventory. Planning a little fat into our inventory in preparation for or in response to product sell-outs is a sure-fire way to end up with lots of excess inventory.

Inventory managers find themselves between a rock and a hard place: Too little inventory results in parts shortages and too much puts a heavy load on business management. This uncomfortable situation has helped give rise to a wonderful concept: "appropriate inventory."

Appropriate inventory means enough inventory to avoid a strain on capital while also avoiding loss of sales due to shortages. It sounds great in theory, but how can appropriate inventory be realized?

There are even some formulas we can use to determine appropriate inventory levels. In one formula, the calculation is based on the sales target. The other is based on cash flow. There are many different formulas expressing different inventory management perspectives.

For example, the following formula is common for sales target-based calculations.

$$\text{APPROPRIATE INVENTORY} = \frac{\text{ANNUAL SALES TARGET (VALUE)}}{\text{MERCHANDISE TURNOVER}}$$

Let's insert some actual figures into this formula by saying that annual sales target (value) equals $32 million and merchandise turnover is 16 times per year.

$$\text{APPROPRIATE INVENTORY} = \frac{\$32 \text{ Million}}{16 \text{ times (per year)}} = \$2 \text{ Million}$$

We can also use these figures to calculate the inventory per merchandise turnover time as follows:

$$365 \text{ days} / 16 \text{ times} = 22.8125 \text{ days}$$

This means a turnover cycle of about 23 days. But is this theory going to work in practice?

In today's wildly erratic markets, how likely is it that any manufacturing company's $32 million sales target will really be that accurate? And how many manufacturers can afford to ignore the considerable impact seasons and climactic changes have on sales? Sales levels are easily influenced by the strategic actions of competitors. And then there is the unpredictability of raw material prices, currency exchange rates, and so on.

Understandably once a company's sales division sets its annual sales target, the sales managers must come up with all sorts of *ad hoc* strategies to actually reach the target. We also need to ask exactly how managers determine the merchandise turnover rate that serves as the denominator in the above formula.

Ordinarily, they use past merchandise turnover rates as their basis for calculation. They then apply various business performance indices as well as the company's current goals in determining the current year's merchandise turnover. These factors change according to the production lead-time and the yield, but they do not change as easily as the sales levels.

So, we can already see that the appropriate inventory is determined using a formula in which both the denominator and the numerator are prone to instability.

Using a formula that divides one unstable factor by another unstable factor to obtain what is treated as a stable value is like trying to divide one negative number by another negative number to obtain a positive number. To put it another way, the appropriate inventory value obtained using the above formula is only as reliable as the unreliable figures used in the formula. (See Figure 2.23.)

Better that we should face the facts: Even if we take the unreliable figures for annual sales and product turnover and temper them with adjustments for estimated seasonal changes, lead-time, and profit ratios, we can still end up with an inventory level that is way off from what turns out to be actually needed.

Figure 2.23   Estimated Appropriateness and Real Appropriateness.

Certainly, it is very important that companies set targets for sales totals, inventory turnover, and other important business performance measures. However, when companies start entrusting these figures to provide them with a prescription for appropriate inventory, it is very easy for them to adopt an attitude of trying to uphold the validity of the figures for the sake of "stability" and at the expense of actual conditions.

Rather than hoping to banish the term "appropriate inventory," I would only hope everyone remembers that *the only really appropriate inventory is zero inventory.*

Lesson 17. The Appropriate Inventory is Zero Inventory

Estimated Lead-Time and Real Lead-Time

Customers are very picky people. They tend to suddenly want products that they never even bothered to look at before. And when they want them, they want them now.

Fashion wear is a prime example of this. Fashion boutiques regularly report cases where some outfit that has stood virtually unnoticed in the window for weeks suddenly starts catching shoppers' interest. Even in the world of food, there is the old saying, "The food that tastes best is whatever you want to eat at the time."

These days, customers are like people who suddenly fall ill in the middle of the night. They may not have seen a doctor in years, but now they need one. Right now, in the middle of the night. There is no time to wait.

A factory's customers rush to order suddenly vital products and want them shipped ASAP. If the factory doesn't fill their needs, they will probably try a different factory next time.

Today, very few factory managers can still afford to tell such customers, "Look, these are all the models we make," or "We'll need at least three months before we can ship it." In a sense, customers have already embraced the Just-In-Time concept: "What I want, when I want it, and in just the amount I want."

Customers end up asking for products to be manufactured and shipped immediately, and factories can only reply, "Sorry, but it takes time to make those things." This creates a gap between customers and manufacturers. Manufacturers have come to regard inventory as something that fills this gap.

We call the period between the customer's placement of an order and the customer's receipt of the product the "customer lead-time." Even if we assume that the factory can begin manufacturing the ordered item right away, this customer lead-time must still include the time needed to make the order. This period is called the manufacturing lead-time. The customer lead-time also includes the time needed to deliver the product, which is called the "transportation lead-time." Let's stop there, omitting any consideration of time needed for clerical work in processing the order, and construct the simple formula:

Customer lead-time = manufacturing lead-time
+ transportation lead-time

Figure 2.24 shows two illustrations based on this formula. However, this lead-time is not short enough to meet the customer's delivery deadline. So let us suppose that the

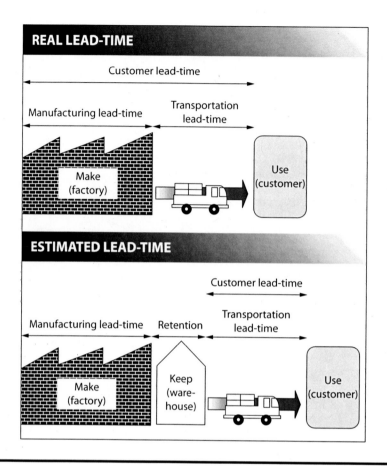

Figure 2.24   Estimated Lead-Time and Real Lead-Time.

company decides to put up a warehouse between its factory and its customers in order to do away with the manufacturing lead-time and enable a shorter "estimated lead-time," whose formula would simply be:

Customer lead-time = transportation lead-time

Here, the warehouse is supposed to make up for the disadvantage of having a manufacturing lead-time. It also means the factory managers can more comfortably plan their production schedules, since they only need to stock that thick wall (the warehouse) between itself and its customers. There is a downside to this scheme, though. The thicker the warehouse wall becomes, the less able the factory is to respond quickly to market changes. That slow response becomes a serious flaw in the factory's character. Production gets stuck in a slow, predictable rut.

It reminds me of the difference we can see between animals who are raised in a zoo and those who never left the wilderness.

Once a factory pursues the inventory option, they do not stop with product inventories. Inventories start piling up between processes or in the assembly line, and then there are the inventories of materials and subcontracted parts.

At each of these inventory sites, a power struggle takes place between the "users" and "providers" of the stocked items. This power struggle is described in the first table.

	User		*Provider*
Product inventory	Market needs	>	Factory's responsiveness
In-process inventory	Capacity of downstream process	<	Capacity of upstream
Materials inventory	Negotiating power and leadership of buyers and outside vendors	<	Resilience of manufacturers

How can we get rid of these inventories? The second table lists different methods to use for different types of inventories.

If manufacturers hope to survive in today's harshly competitive markets, they must learn how to rid themselves of these inventory "buffers" and become more responsive to meeting their customers' short-term demand for everchanging products. Companies make a very big mistake when they depend on something like the above estimated lead-time to meet their customers' needs. A strong, healthy factory is one that can meet needs for prompt delivery based on a real lead-time.

Product inventories	Since market needs cannot be weakened, we have to strengthen the factory's responsiveness to those needs.
In-process inventories	Raise the capacity and flexibility of downstream processes. Do this by thoroughly implementing the "next customer is the customer" concept.
Materials inventories	Strengthen the negotiating power and leadership of buyers and contractors coordinators.

Lesson 18. The Slow-but-Safe Approach Robs Factories of Their Brilliance

Approach to Equipment: Automation and Human Automation (*Jidoka*)

The world is full of automatic machines. As their name implies, almost all of these automatic machines are "self-moving." We just flip the ON switch, and leave the rest up to the machine. Today, there are even automatic machines busy making other automatic machines.

Still, not everything is perfect in robotland. For instance, very few automatic machines have the ability to stop upon detecting defects caused by worn or missing components. Automatic machines that seem to be the ultimate in convenience at one moment can suddenly become mass producers of junk at the next moment.

Obviously, this will not do. The natural response is to put a human inspector on the job to watch out for such sudden quality changes. But the need for a human dilutes the meaning of automatic machines as labor-saving devices, even though this is what has to be done to maintain product quality.

This paradoxical situation gave rise to the idea of *jidoka*, or human automation. *Jidoka* is what enables the machine to be stopped the moment a defect occurs, a machine component breaks, the production flow backs up, or a mistake-proofing alarm goes off. People apply their own human wisdom and

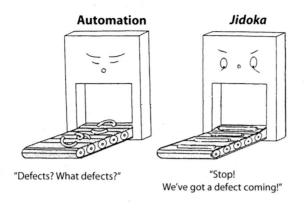

Automation   **Jidoka**

"Defects? What defects?"   "Stop!
We've got a defect coming!"

Figure 2.25   Automation and Human Automation (*Jidoka*).

experience-based "know-how" to equip the machine with devices that are able to detect any of the above conditions and bring it to an immediate stop.

In JIT production, we use the term "automated machine" to refer to machines that, once activated, will run on their own regardless of defects. We use "human automated machine" or "*jidoka* machine" to refer to machines that include "wisdom-based" defect detection improvements, such as those just described. We must always make a clear distinction between these two types of machines. It may be helpful to remember that *jidoka* machines include more value-adding "work" in their operations than do automated machines. (See Figure 2.25.)

> ## Lesson 19. Let's Make Jidoka *Machines That Do All the Human Work*

Improve Work Operations before Improving Equipment

There are basically three types of improvement methods used in JIT improvements. The first is the awareness revolution, the second is improving operations, and the third is improving equipment.

Many people get confused over which method to start with. Some companies are too anxious to exhibit the success of improvement activities and hastily pursue the improvements

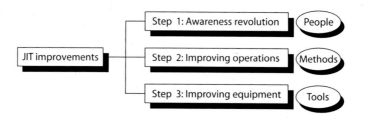

Figure 2.26 Sequences for Carrying Out JIT Production.

that promise the most obvious results. Other companies, under pressure from parent companies to lower costs, go after improvements aimed at drastically lowering prices within a very short time frame, such as two or three months.

There are many ways to approach making improvements, but there is a recommended sequence for carrying out improvements, as shown in Figure 2.26.

The first step is the awareness revolution. The reasons for this can be summed up in two words: people and money.

Production is rooted in people. People build in the defects. People go over the delivery deadline. People push up costs. The starting point for manufacturing is always people. Therefore, we begin by revolutionizing people's awareness.

Building from the ground up, we begin with improving what is most basic—people's perceptions and attitudes—before going on to improve operations and equipment. If we can change people's awareness, we can change their operation habits centered on shish-kabob lot production and can avoid having to waste money on high-priced advanced equipment. But none of these things will change unless we lay the groundwork through the awareness revolution.

Of these three types of improvements—awareness revolution, operations improvements, and equipment improvements—which tends to cost the most money? The answer is obvious: equipment improvements. After that comes operations improvement, and then the awareness revolution, which doesn't need to cost anything at all.

The awareness revolution means helping others realize that conventional lot production no longer makes sense and helping them reach the heartfelt resolution that it is high time to switch to one-piece flow manufacturing. Resolution and determination are free.

Thus, there are two very good reasons for starting with the awareness revolution: people and money.

The term "awareness revolution" is not at all an exaggeration. What we are really talking about here is *revolutionizing* our perceptions and attitudes about manufacturing. JIT improvement is not about finding and correcting errors and misperceptions in our current way of thinking. JIT improvement is plainly radical and revolutionary; it demands that we wholeheartedly discard the conventional wisdom that we have gradually developed over the past two or three decades.

Some people may object, "It'll take too long to revolutionize everyone's awareness." That is a valid objection. It could easily take years to "brainwash" everyone into supporting JIT production.

That is why we begin at the top of the company. If we can get the managers, including the improvement team leaders, to start saying, "Right! Let's get to it!" that will do for starters. Go on to improving operations, and while that is happening, the hands-on experience of making actual improvements will ignite the spark of JIT revolutionary thinking in the participating factory workers.

The second step, as mentioned above, is improving work procedures.

Why put improving work procedures ahead of improving equipment? Again, there are two reasons: money and what we might call "industrial fundamentalism."

By making it perfectly clear where each thing is to be placed during the flow of production, by having clearly defined work methods and advancement methods, and by thoroughly eliminating waste, we can make improvements that will ably serve as the basis for standardized operations.

By contrast, improving equipment consists mainly of introducing new machines and redesigning production lines toward the goal of "workerless automation."

Back to the first reason: money. Which kind of improvement costs more, operations or equipment? Again, the answer is obvious: Improving equipment costs more.

One trap companies barely in the black tend to fall into is jumping into equipment improvements before getting very far with operations improvements. Enthusiastic suggestions such as, "Hey, we really need an NC drilling machine!" or "Let's get a computer to help us automate this line!" are often acted upon prematurely.

I have seen many cases where an improvement team was such only in name. What it really had become was a bunch of equipment procurement consultants! I must admit, it is fun to buy things. Especially if the things you buy are interesting. Everyone naturally gets excited at the chance to follow their interests and buy or build the kind of "toy" they always wanted. It is also a great way to avoid having to "hang in there," putting all your experience and know-how to work in brainstorming improvements.

I have often been asked, "What makes JIT improvements succeed?" There is only one answer: "Going into the red." What I mean by this is that the best approach to making improvements is the poor man's approach—do not spend any money. Once everyone realizes that there is no money to throw at problems, they will start getting serious about using their smarts to improve operations. Money is best kept a forbidden option when improving work procedures.

As mentioned above, the other reason for putting work procedure improvements ahead of equipment improvements is "industrial fundamentalism."

The process of production is a flow that begins with gathering materials and ends with shipping finished products.

The ways in which things are built and advanced along this flow determines the flow itself. These various means within the production flow are called "devices." Improving operations means improving these "flow devices" within the production system.

People are production's main asset and flow devices make up its foundation. Machines and other equipment are just one of the elements that make up the flow devices. They are simply tools that facilitate production.

When we look at production in this manner, how can we possibly justify ignoring the flow devices—the very foundation of production—and instead focus on improving the production tools known as the equipment? But people often make the big mistake of failing to take this "fundamentalist" perspective. Instead, they consider improving the equipment the basic point and then try to adjust the flow devices to suit the improved equipment.

I call this erroneous reasoning the "company cop-out." People realize that to change production's flow devices, they first must change people's attitudes. But changing people's attitudes is much easier said than done. After all, those attitudes are deeply intertwined in the complex web of interdependency that forms part of the company's "character" or "culture."

How much easier it seems to avoid all that awareness revolution hassle and solve the problem with money. This "quick fix" temptation is a major stumbling block, leading to the endless pit known as "plant investment." Quite a few U.S. and European companies have stumbled into that pit. The world's largest automaker and Europe's oldest automaker are among the stumblers.

JIT improvement faces a more hostile environment in Europe and America, where the workers are less motivated and the labor unions more powerful than they are in Japan, which means that Western managers find it harder to influence the corporate character or culture. Pressured by an emphasis on short-term evaluations of their company's business performance, Western managers are even more sorely tempted to use the "company cop-out" and prematurely invest in new equipment.

Japan is more fortunate in that Japanese companies regard their employees as their basic asset. And that is the way it should be: Go straight to employees to improve flow devices. *We need to understand that equipment improvements are appropriate only as a secondary development built upon a solid foundation of improved flow devices.*

Lesson 20. Don't Jump to the Equipment Conclusion!

Five Problems Typically Encountered When Improving Equipment

To sum things up from the previous section, production is rooted in people. We start by focusing on people and on their work as it relates to flow devices for production.

In doing their work related to production flow devices, people invent and introduce tools to facilitate production. Production equipment is among these tools. Remember: First comes the flow devices and next comes the tools. No one would even dream of chartering an airplane for a trip across the street to the neighborhood market. A pair of shoes on your feet will do just fine for that.

The tools change only after the work-related flow devices change. If we have a shish-kabob, large-lot production system, we will want to have equipment suitable for that kind of system. The product's parts may be tiny, but when you put them together into lots of 10, 100, or even 1,000 they can get rather bulky. Such huge production lots require big equipment in order to reach a similarly large scale. Soon we start putting a greater emphasis on how big and fast a machine is rather than on how well it performs its function. Likewise, we start concentrating on the speed of specific processes and lose sight of the overall production flow. Before we know it, we are investing absurd amounts of money in big, advanced equipment.

The basic concept for production flow devices is that *we build using only what we need for one-piece flow manufacturing*. This is the idea that we must keep in mind when deciding what equipment to use.

Admittedly, this idea is not much fun compared to the thought of customizing the production equipment to suit your own fancy and buying new equipment that comes equipped with interesting technologies. I suppose we never really lose that childhood desire to playfully take toys apart or to show off new toys to our friends.

Production engineers and equipment technicians often get together to ask equipment-loving managers for new toys. Managers should be forewarned never to buy equipment just because some people think it would be nifty. It would even be a mistake for managers to pay for the equipment out of their own pockets.

There is something that poses even greater production problems than money: what to do about the production flow once one or more new pieces of equipment have been brought in. And if the new equipment really messes up the production flow, who is going to take responsibility for correcting the situation? Often, the whole factory has to be redesigned in order to find a production flow that can include the new equipment.

Figure 2.27 illustrates five types of problems one can run into when making equipment improvements.

Problem 1: Equipment improvements cost money— A woodworking plant was having trouble with a production bottleneck in its plywood fabrication process. Specifically, pressing the boards was taking too long and the company management decided to scrape the money together to buy a high-frequency press to speed up the pressing time. However, it was only after the press was delivered that they discovered that the previous process (frame-making), which used metal tacks to hold the frames *together, was not compatible with the*

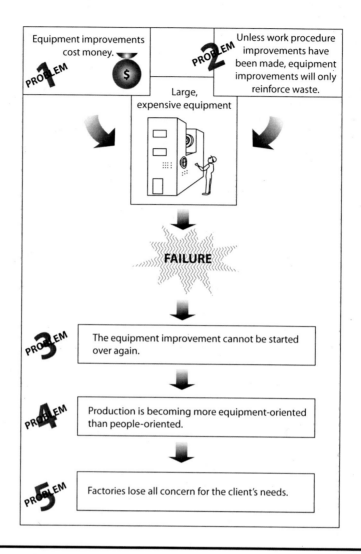

Figure 2.27   Five Types of Equipment Improvement Problems.

high frequency press. As a result, the company was unable to use its expensive new toy.

It is amazing how common these kinds of mistakes are. People tend to think only of specific processes (workers think only of their own) and they do not give much thought to what effects a new piece of equipment's characteristics or design might have on other processes. They also tend to bring new equipment into the production line without first considering what it will mean for the overall line. The result is that expensive equipment gets abandoned because it is difficult, and sometimes impossible, to make it work as part of the production line.

Need we be reminded that the point of improvements is to remove waste, not add to it?

Problem 2: Unless operation improvements have been made, equipment improvements will only reinforce waste—This tale comes from a factory that builds control components. Management had decided to shoot for the goal of a completely automated, "workerless" factory, and had instructed equipment engineers and technicians to analyze the current situation. The plan was to automate the entire factory—from receiving materials to shipping finished products. The company came up with the mega-money needed for this ambitious project, and within six months the equipment was installed and running. The automated equipment churned out products similar in quality to what they had had before. The factory was able to cut its workforce drastically and both the company president and factor superintendent were pleased as punch.

But they overlooked a few things. In order to include five value-adding processes, they needed to lengthen the production line several hundred meters. Most of the new line was occupied by industrial robots that pickup, set down, and otherwise arrange parts. Although it would have been quite possible to have parts soldered in a one-piece flow, the robot system required that parts be arranged into batches of about 20, which the robots dip into a soldering vat. Since the soldering is done in batches, it is hard to achieve consistency. Therefore, management brought in a computer-controlled robot to inspect the soldering.

As you can see, the company neglected removing waste from their old operations, and therefore simply incorporated that invisible waste into the automated system. When waste is due to human operations, it can almost always be removed by improvements in operations. But once the waste is embedded in a complicated set of equipment, it may well be stuck there forever.

This automated production line is accompanied by several hundred meters of in-process inventory The company has also tied up its money in an unmanned material handling system that has absolutely nothing to do with adding value to its products. Suddenly control parts have become a very expensive product to make!

Problem 3: The equipment improvement cannot be started over again—At a diecasting plant, an increase in production volume resulted in a bottleneck at the shotblasting process. The company's solution was to buy a much larger shotblasting machine that could handle several times the current production volume. It was so big and bulky, however, that it had to be placed in another room for use whenever a bottleneck occurred.

Sure, the new shotblasting machine could handle several times the processing load, but to do so required shotblasting diecastings in batches. The diecastings banged into each other while being deburred by the shotblasts, resulting in a great number of damaged, defective diecastings. The factory managers then decided to station two people as quality inspectors responsible for sorting the defective diecastings from the nondefective ones. The amount of stock-on-hand doubled and the big machine's placement in another room required a forklift for conveyance.

Without bothering to first improve the operations, this factory saw its problem simply in terms of insufficient capacity and jumped to the conclusion of installing a larger machine. Waste created more waste because, after installing the large machine, the shotblasting process included more waste (in inspection, conveyance, etc.) than before.

In such cases as this, even when the people concerned realize their mistake and start gnashing their teeth in regret, it is too late: The equipment has been bought and the improvement cannot be started over again.

Problem 4: Production is becoming more equipment-oriented than people-oriented—Even in smaller factories, it is not hard to find such things as large, expensive production machinery and equipment, and multimillion-dollar automated production lines. There are numerically controlled (NC) machines for functions ranging from coating to drying, rinsing, shotblasting, vat soldering, lathing and drilling, and some factories line these advanced machines up in fully automated machining lines or assembly lines. Some companies invest a mint in automated conveyance systems and sophisticated automated warehouses until their factories begin to appear more like conveyance and warehousing centers than manufacturing centers.

These types of equipment improvements cost lots of money, only further embed waste into the production system, and in many cases cannot be rejected as a bad idea once they are installed. Soon, the worst possible thing happens: The factory employees take the attitude, "Well, we bought all this expensive stuff, now we'd better get maximum use out of it." This is an attitude that changes the orientation of factory work away from the workers and places it on the equipment.

Let us imagine, for instance, a factory where the workers have dug a large pit to accommodate a big new machine. Once the machine is installed, there it sits, stuck in one place, as if to proclaim, "No matter what kind of product we switch to, I have to do my work right here."

I am amazed at how inflexible some "flexible automated production lines" actually are. They generally cannot handle a wide range of product models. Consequently, the lots on these lines gradually grow larger and larger.

Problem 5: Factories lose all concern for customer needs—When factory managers grow attached to fixed ideas, such as: "That machine has to stay where it's bolted," "Frequent changeovers reduce efficiency," and, "We've got to increase capacity utilization," the factory's "character" seems to lose all concern for customer needs.

The high cost and irreversibility of equipment improvements are serious problems indeed, yet they are nothing compared to the problem of a company that has become more concerned with its equipment than with its customers' needs.

Lesson 21. Use the Manufacturing Flow to Design the Equipment

Twelve Conditions for Introducing New Equipment

As mentioned earlier, some factories have rushed into buying and installing new equipment in the name of "improvement" or "rationalization" before thinking of how their current operations and methods might first be improved. The managers at these factories bring in new equipment as something separate from the factory's work operations and then, when things do not work out as well as planned, they believe the factory workers are at fault.

This tendency is especially prevalent among the equipment engineering staff at corporate head offices. Knowing precious little about how things are actually made at the factory, these engineers instead study up on the "elegant" functions and advanced technological features of state-of-the-art equipment, and are lured by their interest into encouraging the purchase of large, expensive new machines. Later, when product model changes, quality problems, operational snags, and other problems start cropping up, these engineers typically write a report to their superiors with the verdict that "the factory workers have not yet learned to use the equipment correctly." Guilt invariably lies on the factory floor, not in the engineering department.

Meanwhile, at the factory, the foremen and workers have had no choice but to try their hardest to "get the hang" of using equipment that is in many ways ill-suited for their manufacturing needs. And still it is the factory people, not the engineers, who come under fire from top management. This shows how little the top managers understand the situation.

To help enlighten everyone in this regard, I have put together the following list of 12 guidelines for introducing new equipment. I hope that all equipment engineers at corporate headquarters will read this list, and especially hope that top managers take these guidelines to heart.

Guideline 1: Use today's sale's figures, not next year's forecast figures—Many companies opt to buy new equipment based on one- or two-year projections of how much they can expect to reap in sales revenues. In other words, these companies are counting their chickens before they are hatched. Once they have installed and start using the new equipment, the companies find they have much more production capacity than they need, and have bought into an "overkill" solution for their previous capacity shortages. Yet despite their new capacity for much larger production volume, the volume stays about the same.

In recent years, it has become more difficult for manufacturing companies to forecast sales figures. We are no longer in an era where steady, rapid growth can be taken for granted.

That is why it is imperative that companies be more conservative by introducing only the equipment they need to support profitability based on today's figures. If the volume of orders starts expanding, the company can respond prudently by gradually adding to its small manufacturing cells. Market needs can vary widely, so it is best to introduce equipment conservatively, and only when warranted by current market needs.

Guideline 2: Remain fully committed to one-piece flow manufacturing—Some processes, such as pressing, cleaning, and soldering, naturally lend themselves to processing workpieces in batches. The tendency is to design such processing equipment to handle increasingly larger lots. But this is a mistake.

It seems more rational and easier to opt for batch processing whenever possible, and it seems a sure-fire productivity booster. But we need to remember that presses, rinsers, and such do not manufacture products on their own. Certainly, we can raise the capacity of each of these processes by using them for batch processing, but the result will be an uneven flow and a net *lowering* of production capacity for the overall manufacturing system. Once we begin devoting some equipment to batch processing, we also will find ourselves soon moving toward bigger and bigger machines with ever larger and larger capacities.

No matter how much a particular process can handle and how quickly it can handle it, it will not add to overall profitability if it exceeds the pitch specified by the order shipment schedule. It is far better to have equipment that will reliably turn out quality products one piece at a time in pace with the shipment pitch than to have even the most impressive batch-processing equipment. (One-piece production flow is described further in Chapter 5.)

Guideline 3: Emphasize cycle time over speed—The speed at which the line moves should be directly tied to the specified production volume for that day. Obviously faster production speeds mean higher daily output levels. That fact alone leads many engineers toward faster machines. There are even engineers who virtually equate increased speed with more advance technology.

The amounts specified in customer orders should determine how many minutes or seconds it should take to process parts or quasi products. We call this amount of time the "cycle time" or "pitch" of production, and we should gear our equipment to keep pace with that pitch. (Cycle time is described further in Chapter 10.)

Guideline 4: Make the equipment both versatile and specialized—How many managers have shouted the battle cry "From now on, we're going to have wide variety production!" while rushing out to spend a fortune on expensive general purpose machines? Once the factory actually starts using one of these do-it-all machines, it finds that change-overs do not go very smoothly and that the machine has various other restrictions, so that the productivity gain is not what everyone had expected. Often, these general purpose

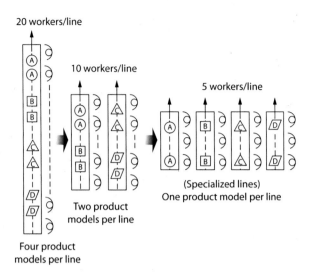

Figure 2.28   Specialized Lines to Meet Wide Variety Production Needs.

machines, which are supposed to do everything, do not do anything particularly well.

But suppose, for instance, that we have a manufacturing line staffed by 20 workers. If we are running four product types through this line, we can split the line in half, with each half operated by 10 workers and specializing in two of the four product models. Alternatively, we could even split the original line into four lines with five workers apiece, and each line could specialize in just one product model. This is a much better way to meet the need for wide variety production. (See Figure 2.28.)

This principle works the same way for individual machines. Get rid of the general purpose machines with their waste-ridden hodgepodge of functions. Instead, stick to inexpensive machines that can be used as specialized machines but can also be made versatile enough to handle product model changes.

Guideline 5: Keep equipment compact and readily movable—With any hope, the days are numbered for huge machines that get plopped down for eternity in one place as if to say, "This is where I stay no matter what product we switch to!" New products are being developed all the time, and the product diversification trend is still gaining momentum.

Factories are learning that the most efficient equipment layout is the one that suits the current product models. The grouping of equipment into in-line patterns requires equipment that is both compact and furnished with casters or other devices for easy movability.

Guideline 6: Make equipment easy to operate and keep machine work and human work separate—We can never get far in training workers in the various skills needed to handle several machines if the machines are so "user hostile" that it takes a "an old hand" to handle them correctly. Likewise, machines that require constant nursing and supervision are hardly conducive to production efficiency.

Instead, the machines should be easily operable by any worker and the workers should be able to physically separate themselves from the machines while the machines are running. Only then are the machines appropriate for multi-process handling. The basic rule for workers being trained in multi-process handling is that this work is chair-free. They must stand (or walk) while working.

Guideline 7: Workpieces should enter and exit each machine at the same spot—Often, machines—especially woodworking machines—take unprocessed workpieces in one side of the machine, process them, and expel them on the other side. Such an arrangement stands in the way of both single-worker handling and multi-process handling by usually requiring a worker on one side to feed workpieces into the machine, and a second worker on the other side to take out the processed workpieces.

To avoid this situation, the workpiece must either be processed in a fixed position or must be automatically returned to the entry point after processing. The best-designed machines are those that support "set-up, set-up work" or "remove, remove work" (in which the worker either sets up or removes a series of workpieces at a series of machines) by expelling each processed workpiece or leaving it where it is, if it is easily extractable.

Guideline 8: Build in inspection functions—Automated machines that are simply automated—meaning they just move by themselves—will keep on moving even after they begin turning out defective products. Before long, there is a large pile of defective junk in front of the machine. To avoid this, we need to turn machines that simply "move" on their own into machines that really "work" on their own.

We can do this by installing *poka-yoke* (mistake-proofing) devices that can "inspect" (detect) when the first defective product has been made or can sometimes even detect when the first one is about to be made. Once these devices detect a defect, they shut off the machine. (*Poka-yoke* is described further in Chapter 12.)

Guideline 9: Keep defective and nondefective products easily countable—In the case of inspection devices for semiconductors and other high-precision products, it is especially helpful to keep defective and nondefective units clearly separated and countable at a glance.

Guideline 10: Make equipment easy to maintain—Regrettably, there are many engineers who seem to only care about how well machines build or process products. Obviously, that is a good thing to care about, but if the machine is going to be a reliable workhorse over time, it needs to be user friendly for maintenance workers. The idea is to give full consideration to both the machine's work functions and its maintainability.

Guideline 11: Keep a clean machine—One does not need to visit too many factories to find machines that are oozing oil or that are surrounded by scattered processing debris. Aside from frequent sweeping and cleaning in line with the "5S" doctrine, shop floor workers need to pinpoint what things are causing the mess and improve them. After all, the 5S's are much easier to maintain if the equipment barely makes a mess to begin with!

Guideline 12: Make sure the equipment keeps you informed—*Poka-yoke* devices are not enough: After detecting a defect and shutting down, each machine should also be able to light an *andon* (alarm lamp) and/or sound a buzzer to let the operators know something has happened. Together, *poka-yoke* and *andon* enable both visual and auditory control.

Lesson 22. Think of Machines as Living Things

Approach to Inspection and Management: Sampling Inspection and Full Lot Inspection

The following describes something that happened at a QC meeting held in a certain factory.

The company was having no luck reducing the steady stream of defect claims and other complaints from its customers. It had tried hanging big banners with QC slogans such as "Quality First" and "This Month Is Quality Assurance Month," but to no avail. Its whole QC effort was just one big defeat. The customer complaints had even *increased* since beginning its QC campaigns.

The factory superintendent spoke out loudly. "We must double our inspection staff and approach this thing more rationally!" he said.

Perhaps the superintendent had grown cynical about the whole affair. But his suggestion was serious, although fundamentally flawed.

Already, we can identify two misunderstandings held by the group. The first is the notion that inspection somehow eliminates defects. No matter how many quality inspectors you put in the factory, the defects are already built into the products long before the inspectors spot them. Defects are results. Clamping down on these "defect" results will not reduce them. At best, such a move will succeed only in screening out the major defects and marginally reducing customer complaints. The point they missed is that defects must not be built into the products in the first place.

Their second misunderstanding concerns the real meaning of "rational." Each product passes through the care of many people on its journey from factory to market and finally to the customer. Each of these people may have a different idea of what is rational.

Some may reason that full lot inspection just takes too much time and statistical studies have shown that sampling inspections do the job well enough. This belief about inspections is especially popular in factories. Many factory workers will vehemently assert that sampling inspection is by far the most rational way to inspect products.

The truth is that they do not know the truth.

The truth is that "rational" is a very treacherous term. It means "compatible with reason." But, as alluded to above, perceptions of reason differ from person to person. In fact, it is nearly impossible to find a common perception of reason shared by everyone. So the problem is that one person's reason might be another person's folly. There is no way to satisfy both of them.

What kinds of people are likely to find sampling inspection a reasonable idea? For starters, the people in the factory are bound to find it reasonable. After all, who in a factory likes the job of rooting out defective products? They would much rather have to apologize now and then for shipped defects than to take all the time and trouble to perform full lot inspections.

Figure 2.29 illustrates a common situation: a factory that has decided it could live with an Acceptable Quality Level (AQL) of 0.1 percent, which means an average of one defective product per 1,000 products.

Production people are proud to report an AQL of "only" 0.1 percent. But from the customer's perspective, that means that the company is happy to sell a lemon to one unlucky customer per thousand! The unlucky customers will not start smiling again when they consider the company's 99.9 percent nondefective rate. He or she is too busy regretting the purchase of a 100 percent defective product.

Figure 2.29   Estimated Quality.

Remember this: One little "oops" by the maker brings one big "ouch" to the buyer. Sampling inspections go with the odds. The odds are good, but not nearly good enough to avoid having losers. Factories that are market-oriented never stray from taking the customers' perspective in their approach to manufacturing their products.

The so-called rational approach works great in general. But we need to consider how rational our approach seems to the individual customer.

Naturally, countless factory managers counter the above with, "Yeah, but do you know what switching to full-lot inspection would do to our costs?" Yes, I know. But then again, 100 percent quality—more than anything else—separates the manufacturing amateurs from the true professionals. After all, what are all those "expert" production engineers for? What is the whole field of industrial engineering for if not 100 percent quality?

Lesson 23. Quality is Built into Products at Each Process

Monitoring and Managing

I cannot recall how many times I have had discussions such as the following with top managers at manufacturing companies.

> "We don't know what to do. We can't seem to increase our control level at all. We can't even get a handle on all the in-process inventory between the process stations."
>
> "Hmmm. Tell me more."
>
> "It's just that we want to gain a better understanding of what is going on and somehow manage to control it in a more timely way. But how can we start doing that?"
>
> "Well, sounds like I'd better teach you the best way to do that." (This last remark always ignites an eager sparkle in their eyes.) "Let's totally eliminate inventory between processes. Down to zero."

The managers invariably greet that last remark by dropping their jaw and staring in wide-eyed amazement. It is not what they expect to hear—not even close, in fact. They expect me to say things like, "Let's make better use of computers. We'll install network monitors all over the factory so we can immediately enter data to keep track of how operations are going and where the inventory is moving."

But the real solution is simply not that complicated.

When managers express the desire to "have better control," they are admitting a failure to understand how factory operations proceed and why they slow down at times. They are also admitting that they have not clearly identified the causes of various shop floor problems, such as product defects and excess between-process inventory. To solve these problems, they imagine it necessary to build a new, more sophisticated factory management and control system, even though building and maintaining such a system will cost a fortune and take untold months or years of effort. Ironically, the end result will be a production system that has become even more complicated and thus more difficult to understand.

Take a look around any large factory and see how many signs include the word "control" or "management." Such signs are everywhere. There is "production management" to manage the entire production system, "financial management" to manage the money, "personnel management" for the employees, "sales management" to keep an eye on the market, and various other self-explanatory types of management or control, such as "client order management," "process control," "delivery management," "quality control," "subcontract management," "cost management," "inventory control," "in-process inventory control," "shipment management," and so on.

One could easily gain the impression that people in manufacturing are embracing the concepts of "control" and "management" like some kind of security blanket.

Some deliveries have been late. What does the company do? It creates a "delivery management" system, replete with a "deadline monitoring system" to monitor whether or not current delivery deadlines are kept.

Some defects occur. Quality is the lifeblood of the company, so the managers make a big fuss about developing a "QC organization," again replete with a "quality monitoring system" to continually keep track of defect occurrences.

What? Too much inventory? Time to set-up an inventory control organization, replete with...

And so it goes. Figure 2.30 provides an amusing illustration of how "monitoring" gets mixed up with "managing" (especially in Japanese, where both words are pronounced *kanri*).

In other words, when factory managers (monitors?) find a problem, they tend to respond by adding the word "management" or "control" to the name of the problem. They put off for later the idea of looking into what actually caused the problem to occur and what can be done to correct the situation.

Figure 2.30   Monitoring (*kanri*) and Management (*kanri*).

Still, almost all managers have this proclivity toward attaching the security-blanket words "management" and "control." The more "management" and "control" systems they create in response to problems, the higher costs rise. I suppose we could call such costs "security-blanket costs."

If these managers would instead channel that same energy toward repeatedly asking, "Why did that problem occur?" until they reach the real root of the problem, they would already be halfway toward implementing improvements to correct the situation.

In most factories, inventory (warehouse inventory, in-process inventory, and between-process inventory) is like a huge, thick blanket that covers up a panorama of causes for problems. If they could only pull that blanket away, all sorts of causes would suddenly become visible. Yank away the cover of in-process and between-process inventory, and suddenly it is obvious how poorly organized the production system is and what can be done to start preventing defects.

Therefore, the first thing to do is reduce inventory to zero. Next, make improvements to solve the most serious problems that suddenly appear. Then redesign the entire production system so that materials fed into the system can be sent through it smoothly—without any retention—to become finished products.

Some people who still have not completely caught on to this idea might still be wondering, "Once we've gotten all that inventory out of there, don't we need to set-up a management system to control the timely flow of inventory?"

To those people, I simply say, "If you have inventory, you need inventory control. If you don't have inventory, you don't need inventory control."

Another way to put this is: The best type of management removes the need for management. We might observe just as accurately that management systems and organizations, once established, have a life of their own.

I could cite case after case in which companies whose scope and volume of business were steadily shrinking still kept their management divisions as big as ever. Management organizations know how to grow, but do not know how to shrink.

Parkinson's Law is alive and well.

Lesson 24. Keep Monitoring Out of Managing

Approach to Promoting Improvements: Pseudo Improvement and Real Improvement

Here is an exchange I once had with a factory employee while starting to implement JIT improvements:

"Hey, what's all this?" I asked, pointing to a pile of cardboard. "Oh, that's the cardboard we use to box up Product A."

I knew right away what kind of beginner's mind-set I was dealing with. Did this person really think I didn't know what cardboard was? Did he think that I was touring the factory to learn about the products they were making? A JIT-minded person would recognize immediately that I was really asking, "Why is this pile of inventory here?" I turned and left that workshop. The people there did not have the slightest idea what JIT improvements meant. It was a waste of time at that point. This person was a rank beginner, a "white belt" in the martial art of JIT improvement.

At other workshops, people had a somewhat better understanding of JIT. When I asked the same question to one worker, he said, "We don't have anywhere to put that stuff right now, so we're keeping it there just for now."

He was beginning to get the idea. But he should have realized I was not interested in hearing excuses. I wanted to know what they were going to do to remove the pile of inventory.

A somewhat more advanced beginning JIT student would say something like, "Right. We'll get right to it," and then make a note of it. The attitude is correct: Acknowledge the problem, then write a memo. Now we are getting somewhere. I would give that person a beginner's black belt.

A still more advanced JIT beginner would get out the memo pad and make a note of it while acknowledging the problem with a simple "Right" or "Got it." Then he would issue an improvement instruction and have the improvement made as soon as possible. Then he would check up on the improvement and make any overlooked items the next items for improvement. Acknowledge, act, and follow up. That puts this person in the second rank of black belts.

Unlike the JIT white belts, the JIT black belts knew how to go about making improvements as soon as the inventory pile was pointed out to them. This makes the difference between "pseudo improvement" and "real improvement." Let us take another look at this important distinction.

Improvement item pointed out—"What's with this pile of stuff here?" (points toward in-process inventory).

Pseudo improvement

The worker seems confused at first when the problem is pointed out. He would not be so confused if he knew what he was doing. But since he does not understand what JIT improvements really are, he feels a vague sense of guilt as if he were lazy or not doing things right. Still ignorant of how to make real JIT improvements, he starts making pseudo improvements.

He scans the walls for a large enough space, where he puts together some shelves. He then moves the pile of stuff from the floor to the shelves. A look of pride appears on his face as he claps the dust off his hands. This man is clearly a "white belt." If possible, he should be downgraded to an even lower rank should he have the inclination to tell a JIT inspector, "I made an improvement."

Real improvement

As soon as the problem is pointed out, the factory employee gets right on it. During the next two or three minutes, he asks a series of "Why?" questions to get to the root cause of the problem. This questioning process is *a must* for making real improvements. We call the process the 5W1H method, in which we need to ask "Why?" at least five times to get to the real cause, then we ask "How?" in order to make the improvement.

The pseudo improvement, in which my question, "What's with this pile of stuff here?" prompted the worker to build shelves and move the stuff to the shelves, the worker's "improvement" made the workshop appear neater but it also grants approval to the pile of inventory by "enshrining" it on specially-built shelves. Instead of removing inventory-related waste, this approach only adds permanence to it.

The 5W1H method is a radically different approach that brings real improvements. We begin this approach by simply asking "Why?" as in, "Why did that pile of inventory accumulate there?" This brings a response, such as, "The people at the previous process have been putting their deliveries there."

At this point, some people might rush into a pseudo improvement, saying," Well, let's build some shelves and get that stuff off the floor!" as a simple (actually, simplistic) solution to the problem.

But that is not the right approach. Instead, we need to ask "Why?" again, as in, "Why do the people at the previous process put their deliveries there?" Let us suppose the response this time is, "Because they're done with it." Now one important fact has surfaced: The factory is using the "push" production method. We have found the basis for an improvement plan: The factory needs to switch from "push" to "pull" production.

But we are still not done asking "Why?" at least five times. The third "Why?" might be, "Why is the previous process producing so much stuff?" The response to that could be, "They can't send the workpieces downstream one at a time," or "They have to process batches for economy's sake."

Each of these responses should be addressed by a fourth "Why"? To the first response, we can ask, "Why can't they send them one at a time?" and, to the second response, "Why is it uneconomical to get rid of batch processing?" Let us suppose the response to both of these questions is, "Because the changeovers take so much time." This brings another problem to the surface: the need to improve changeovers at the previous process. (See Figure 2.31.)

While this and the "shelving solution" are both improvements, one is just a pseudo improvement and the other is real improvement. No matter how much thought, action, time, and expense go into a pseudo improvement, it will not improve the workplace a bit. Only by getting to the bottom

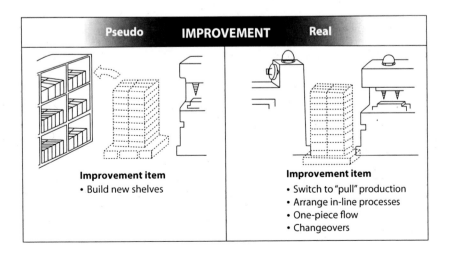

Figure 2.31   Pseudo Improvement and Real Improvement.

of the problem through the 5W1H method can we make sure our improvements are real ones.

The "white belt" workers who do not know how to make *real* improvements need to be handed a 5W1H sheet and told what to do with it. (See Figure 2.32.)

Lesson 25. 5W1H

"Mental" Improvements and "Physical" Improvements

This JIT manual includes explanations of the things most essential to JIT improvements in factories:

- JIT's basic concepts
- Improvement techniques and their functions
- Improvement "know-how" and case studies

JIT improvement consultants make use of know-how that they have accumulated over many years.

Some aspiring students of JIT may imagine that if they read this manual cover-to-cover without overlooking a single word or phrase, they can expect to be full-fledged JIT improvement consultants when they close the back cover. The same thing may happen in companies with industrial engineers. They may read this manual and then fancy themselves veteran JIT/IE professionals. As soon as these people put this book down, they will be off preaching the JIT gospel to others.

Let us nip this potential disaster in the bud right now. *JIT improvement is not a theory or technique.* JIT improvement is a discipline, one might even say an art, that is based at first on faith and then, gradually, on accumulated experience, wisdom, and intuitive "gut feelings." JIT improvement is a process, a path leading toward revolutionary progress in manufacturing, and this manual is nothing more than an entry and basic guide to that path.

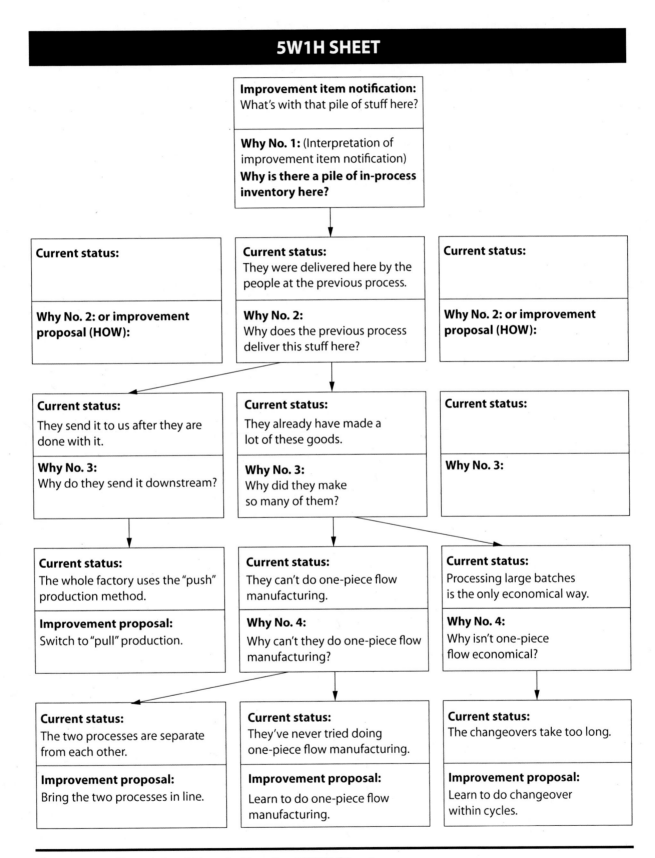

Figure 2.32 **Example of How to Use the 5W1H Sheet.**

JIT improvement expertise cannot be garnered from books. Neither can it be learned by talking about it or by listening to others talk about it.

Several years ago, TQC was all the rage in Japanese manufacturing circles. In fact, the TQC movement spread from factories to hospitals and even government offices.

Its application scope seemed boundless.

TQC had a lot going for it. After all, there is nothing at all wrong with asking everyone in the company to brainstorm solutions to problems and make improvements. However, the result was often long on form and short on substance. It became obvious that people were aiming their improvement efforts toward a impressive announcement meeting rather than toward substantial changes in the workplace.

JIT improvement eliminates all emphasis on formalities and announcement meetings.

Factories that have embraced TQC often become wall-to-wall displays of advocatory posters, signboards, and banners emblazoned with such popular TQC slogans as "Orderliness and Cleanliness," "Let's Raise Productivity," "Let's Reduce Inventory," and "The Next Process Is Your Customer."

Nothing gets improved in factories full of TQC posters. Or perhaps I should say that factories get filled up with TQC posters because nothing gets improved.

I remember seeing a factory floor where a "Let's Reduce Inventory" banner that hung from the ceiling was partially hidden by a huge heap of inventory. That is what happens when form becomes more important than substance.

JIT improvements are not a set of slogans to be written here and there.

TQC makes use of the "Seven QC Tools." One of these tools is the Pareto chart, which is often used to analyze defects. These charts quite legibly indicate the type and number of defects and are drawn very neatly Then they are posted in the factory so everyone can read them. This is all fine and good, but it is unfortunate indeed what often happens afterward. People start reading the charts as if they were lottery results or TV game-show competitions, saying, "Hey, look who scored number one in defects this week!" After a while, it gets hard to tell the best from the worst.

People also tend to get distracted from the real point of the charts by their natural tendency to admire the craftsmanship of its carefully drawn illustrations. This unfortunate tendency to channel the seven QC tools toward making impressive statistical displays for people to admire instead of making full-fledged improvement efforts has prompted the invention of a nickname for QC's seven tools: QC fireworks.

JIT improvement gets rid of the flash and bang of TQC and keeps things pure and simple. JIT improvement is not about seeing, reading, talking, listening, mathematizing, announcing, or writing. It is about *improving*.

So how can we properly define JIT improvement? My suggestion is that JIT improvement is factory-based improvement toward the realization of JIT production. These factory-based improvements are not primarily based on reading, writing, or even seeing. As their name implies, they are about improving factories.

JIT improvement emphasizes only one verb: doing. (See Figure 2.33.)

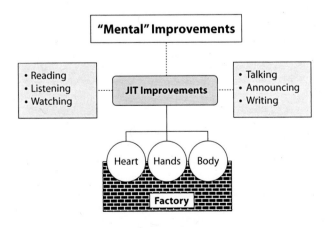

Figure 2.33 **"Mental" Improvement and "Factory" Improvement.**

In JIT improvements, we just show up at the factory and get cracking. Everyone immediately starts using their wits and their bodies to make improvements.

Everything involved in making the improvement happens right there at the factory. Each person is on his or her feet and stays standing for hours, if necessary. If we stay on our feet and remain focused on the factory itself, the factory will be the teacher, providing the ideas and clues needed to start making improvements.

The factory itself will softly whisper into our ears such invaluable teachings as the movement of the machines, the flow of goods, the items in need of improvement. To be able to hear these barely audible whispers, we need to stand very calmly and explore the factory with deep interest. As we do this, we gradually and naturally acquire skill in identifying such things. We need to do what we can to foster this skill.

Nothing could be more foolish than launching improvement campaigns from desks and blackboards. In study rooms, we have to rely on our mental pictures of the factory. That leaves too much of a gap between what we remember and what conditions actually exist in the factory. When improvements are based on such mental images instead of the factory itself, the result can only be disappointment and despair.

People who have had more than the average number of years in academia tend to fall into the bad habit of making such "mental" improvements. In seeking to make improvements, we must use the body—not the mind—as the main perceptive instrument. We need to feel as if we had cut off our own heads and sent them home for a while.

Lesson 26. The Factory Is the Best Teacher of Improvements

Bottom-up Improvements and Top-down Improvements

Generally, there are two ways to make things better.

One way is to meticulously research current conditions and methods, analyze the research results, then improve the problem points. This is the inductive method. The other way is to state the ideal conditions and methods, and gradually improve current conditions until they approximate the ideal. This is the deductive method. Whenever people speak of "improvement," they are speaking of at least one of these two methods. The inductive method is the conventional industrial engineering (IE) method. The deductive method is the JIT improvement method.

The conventional IE method is an attempt to raise the level of quality based on a thorough analysis of current conditions. It is thus a "bottom-up improvement" method.

By contrast, the JIT improvement method takes the ideal of "JIT production" as the basis or final cause for making improvements. It is thus a "top-down improvement" method. Actually, the ideal at the top does not go down in any way but is used to pull conditions upward, and so it would be more precise to call JIT a "top-up improvement" method. For simplicity's sake, it is better to keep a sharp contrast with IE's bottom-up approach by calling the JIT approach "top-down improvement."

The same contrast in methods can be seen in other fields, too. For instance, in budgetary accounting there is the "build-up method" and the "zero-base method." In price setting, there is the "cost-based method" and the "market value method." In systems design, there is the "analytical system design" method and the "work design" method.

Perhaps the closest analogy to factory improvement is child rearing. Here, the two methods are the "faultfinding" method, in which the child is scolded for everything he or she does wrong, and the "dream-instilling" method, in which the vision of achieving a future goal or hope is deeply instilled in the child.

It is not always easy to say which factory improvement method is better—the IE method or the JIT method. It depends very much on the company. However, we must not lose sight of the critical need for companies to root out bad habits and make fundamental changes to survive in today's world of trade friction, fluctuating exchange rates, and severe competition.

Such radical change does not come from "improvements" in the ordinary sense of the word, that is, in small, incremental improvements. Instead, such companies require innovation and revolutionary changes. And for making those kinds of changes, the conventional IE method is difficult indeed.

What makes the IE method so difficult is that, as a method based on analysis of current conditions, it must begin with "recognizing" and therefore to some degree "accepting" current conditions. We study the status quo in order to make it a little bit better, but we never ask the radical question, "Why are things the way they are?"

For example, consider a factory that has a conveyance system. To make just one improvement in this system, we must take totally different approaches depending upon whether we use the IE method or the JIT method.

If we use the conventional IE method, we begin by carefully analyzing the conveyors and the way things are distributed by them. We can then note that the conveyors place some items in sites from where they can easily be removed and other items in less accessible sites. We can graphically analyze this phenomenon in a "conveyor use index" chart. The chart plots items that are left piled on the floor as the lowest value in optimum conveyor use and items that are still being moved on the conveyor as the highest value in optimum conveyor use. As shown in the graph in Figure 2.34, there are five levels of conveyor use including the lowest and highest just described.

Using the IE method, we identify the low points on the analyzed use index and seek to improve them to have higher use levels (therefore easier to convey), so that the overall average use index becomes higher.

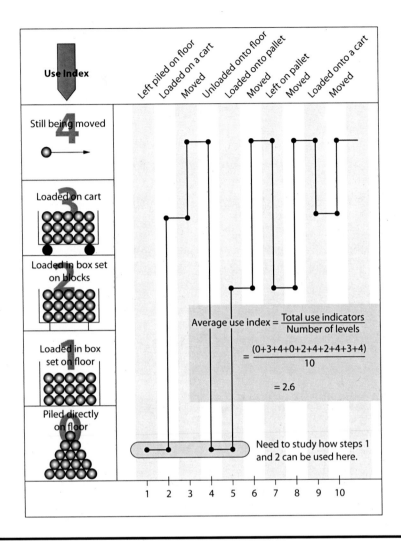

Figure 2.34 Conveyor Use Index (IE Method).

To be sure, this sort of improvement should help goods flow more smoothly, and if they actually do flow more smoothly, that itself can be expected to have positive effects.

However, this improvement method falls short of asking the radical "Why?" question: Why does this conveyor system have to exist? Therefore, it is not a revolutionary method. Instead, it accepts the conveyance system as a *fait accompli* and goes directly to attempting improvements in it.

I know of many factories that have thoroughly implemented this conventional IE approach. In every one of these factories, roller conveyors have been installed between every process. Conveyors cover these factories like so many cold, black carpets. In-process inventory is set upon these narrow conveyors. The utmost goal of the IE method for improving these conveyors is to raise their average use index to the highest use level. Beyond that, the IE method envisions nothing in the way of further improvements.

Now let us examine how we might apply the JIT method in one of these factories. We would begin by getting rid of all of the roller conveyors. Why? Because, as mentioned earlier, the JIT method regards improvements to an existing conveyor system as "pseudo improvements," which JIT professionals avoid like the plague.

After getting rid of the roller conveyors, the JIT method calls for the creation of a new factory layout and new work methods that allow production to proceed without any conveyance system at all. If such improvements are made, the factory will be rendered free of any need for conveyance and its attendant problems.

As you can see, both of these methods (IE and JIT) are called "improvement methods," but that is about all they have in common.

JIT is so revolutionary that some people have half-seriously suggested it is a religion. Perhaps it is. Like most religions, JIT offers an ideal state of being (for factories, at least) and challenges the factories to try to attain that state. But there is nothing evangelical about JIT. If anything, JIT is an inner-directed, contemplative "religion" that asks its followers to focus on their own companies, factories, workplaces, and selves. JIT begins with a quiet introspection into all of these things. If it has any close cousin in the field of religion, it would probably be the Japanese Zen sect that sprang from contemplative Buddhist sects in India and China.

JIT has no set organizational structure or "how to" manual. No doubt this makes the goal of approximating JIT production all the more difficult. When people hear this, they often ask, "So what is the best way to carry out JIT improvements?"

To this frequent question, I have two answers up my sleeve. One is, "Go into the red." In other words, take the poor man's approach to making improvements and spend as little money as possible.

The other answer is, "Believe in JIT." This answer goes especially to top managers, for it is they who must first believe in JIT in order to get middle managers and their subordinates to believe. Although belief in JIT must start with top managers, its most essential believers are the factory employees. If they truly believe in JIT, they will make big improvements in their factories.

I should also add that the goal of JIT production should never be far from the hearts and minds of everyone. Getting there requires faith.

Lesson 27. Keep JIT in Mind and Apply Improvements to Yourself

"Yes" and "Yes, I'll Do It Right Away"

Day-to-day life is awash in information, provided via such media as newspapers, books, radio, television, and so on. As a result, we all have second-hand knowledge about a wide variety of subjects.

For example, you or I may not be athletic in the least, but if we watch sports programs on television, we come to understand a lot about certain sports without having to actually go out and run, jump, or sweat. Likewise, some people develop a strong sense of affinity and familiarity with foreign lands and peoples based solely on what they have read in travel literature or have seen on TV.

We can find the same kind of people in the field of JIT improvements. People who have never even set foot in a factory will confidently explain such things as flow production to their friends. Such people have achieved some skill at "mental improvements," but have no experience at all in "physical improvements."

I do not know how many times I have heard discussions and debates on JIT improvement that include nothing but "mental improvements." Mental improvements, no matter how skillful and eloquent they may be, are of no help at all in the real world of physical improvements. Mental improvements are devoid of value unless they are followed up by a trip to the factory, long and diligent efforts, and results that are seen and felt physically.

Second-hand knowledge is useless for JIT improvements. JIT improvements need hands-on learning.

Let us take an imaginary trip through a factory that is currently undergoing some improvements. Right now we are standing in front of a manufacturing cell where an important improvement—switching to flow production—has just been made.

"You have a U-shaped cell now, so you've got to stop working with lots."

Even a simple instruction such as this one spurs different reactions at different workplaces. The reaction is a good indication of how fully the JIT improvement method has been accepted and incorporated. I have been able to delineate seven stages of JIT acceptance, as illustrated in Figure 2.35.

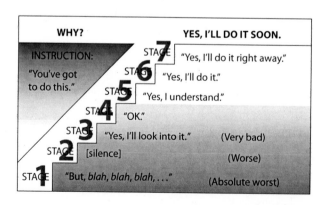

Figure 2.35 Seven Stages in the Acceptance of the JIT Improvement Method.

Stage 1: "But, *blah, blah, blah...*"

Excuse-making is the worst possible response. It would be better not to say anything than to try to make excuses. During a factory visit, I can tolerate about three excuse-makers if I am in an exceptionally good mood, but if my mood is not so expansive, even one excuse-maker is enough to convince me that the factory is not worth any more of my time. I'm not at all interested in visiting factories where the people are only pretending to be carrying out JIT improvements.

Stage 2: [silence]

There are actually two types of silent responses. One is when the person is too wrapped up in trying to figure out how to make the improvement to say anything, and the other is when the person is just plain put off by the instruction.

The first kind of silence is OK, though not exactly polite, but the second kind is very bad indeed. The person who responds this way usually lacks perseverance and patience, resists change, and harbors resentment against those who propose changes. JIT leaders are always being "stabbed in the back" by this type of person. Rather than feel the chill wind blowing through the knife holes in his or her back, it is better that the JIT leader just find the nearest exit.

Stage 3: "Yes, I'll look into it."

This can be seen as the total opposite to the silent response at the second stage. The respondent sounds upbeat and attentive. But the chances are that he or she is making an empty promise. I have learned that you can trust a factory worker who says, "I'll look into it," about as much as you can trust a typical politician who says, "I'll be sure to address that problem." They might as well be saying, "OK, I won't do a thing."

On my next visit, I usually voice a short, sarcastic remark such as, "My, you folks are really doing a lengthy study of this problem," before moving directly to the next workshop.

To sum things up so far, the three bad responses are: "But *blah, blah, blah*," "[silence]," and "Yes, I'll look into it." Factories where such responses are common are on the fast track to Nowhere as far as JIT improvement is concerned. To get back on the right track and survive as a business, they need to launch a company-wide campaign to abolish such counterproductive attitudes to make room for JIT improvement to firmly take root.

Stage 4: "OK."

Like a silent response, a simple "OK" can have more than one meaning. It may seem like a simple and total acceptance of the instruction, but it is not very good communication. One cannot tell, for instance, whether the meaning is, "Yes, the current way is wrong," or "Yes, you're right." A more precise answer that reflects the respondent's meaning would be better.

Stage 5: "Yes, I understand."

While not as bad as a too simple and too vague "OK," this response still suffers from vagueness.

Improvements are not primarily something to be "understood" intellectually. They are things to be *done* in the factory. Understanding them without doing them means nothing. In fact, it is *only by doing them* that we can really understand them. So, I usually meet this response with something like, "After you've made the improvement, I'll be able to see whether you understood it or not."

Stage 6: "Yes, I'll do it."

When the person immediately gives this response, you know he or she has cleared a big hurdle. It is very big step indeed to get from a simple "Yes" to an energetic, "Yes, I'll do it."

There is only one hurdle left: the question of when it will get done. Obviously, if the respondent's intention is to get it done about six months from now, he or she has not really made it to Stage 6 after all.

Stage 7: "Yes, I'll do it right away."

During a factory visit, when I give even the mildest kind of instruction and hear this sincere response, I know I am dealing with a JIT champion who has taken the JIT improvement method to heart.

When the typical type of response in a factory improves from "Yes," to, "Yes, I'll do it," and finally, "Yes, I'll do it right away," I can tell just how far the people have come in understanding JIT. After all, JIT is almost synonymous with "doing it right away."

Lesson 28. Attitude Adjustment:
From "Yes" to "Yes, I'll Do It Right Away"

A Passion for Improvement

JIT improvement includes more than building a few custom-made jigs and removing waste from operations. Obviously, these small improvements can add up to something big and are a key part of JIT improvement. But the real gist of JIT improvement is the discarding of old ideas and habits, changing over to flow production, and otherwise overhauling the entire factory until it becomes a factory that efficiently serves the current needs of the marketplace. This amounts to nothing short of a factory revolution and a major innovation in the way to conduct business.

JIT improvement rightfully stands among the ranks of other movements that have resulted in major business innovations. JIT turns factory improvements into innovations. The most important prerequisite for innovation is *enthusiasm.* The ability to remain constantly enthusiastic—something we admire in young people—is a vital part of the JIT improvement approach.

But what about the over-30 set? How are they supposed to keep up their enthusiasm?

One good way is to put some psychological distance between ourselves and our workplace. When a series of

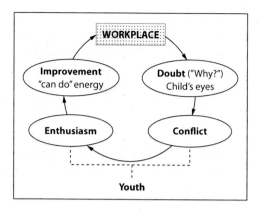

Figure 2.36   JIT Improvement (Innovation) Cycle.

problems occurs in the workplace and cause disorder, we need to be detached and objective enough to look at the situation with a child's eyes and ask the typical child's question: "Why?" The more we lose this ability to wonder and ask "Why?" the harder it becomes to revolutionize the factory and its long-established traditions.

After we learn to keep wondering and asking "Why?" we come to the next hurdle: dealing with difficult problems. This is the time for brainstorming. It is also the time when conflicts begin.

If we rub two objects together, we get friction. Likewise, friction also may occur in the human mind when improvement ideas rub up against current habits. It gets people's dander up, but by the same token, it can also get their enthusiasm up. If we can keep fanning the flames of this enthusiasm, all we need after that is the determination and strength to revolutionize the factory. Then we just do it.

This entire process moves in cycles: First we go to the workplace, then we look around with a child's eyes and ask, "Why?" Next, we confront conflict and fire up our hearts with youthful enthusiasm, then we pour our energy into making the improvements. This cycle is called "the JIT Improvement (Innovation) Cycle." (See Figure 2.36.)

Lesson 29. Improvement Is Enthusiasm

Index

1973 oil crisis, 8
3 Mu's, 643
    eliminating, 151
5 Whys and 1 How, 24, 128, 129, 130–134
    waste discovery by, 208–210
5MQS waste, 152–153
    conveyor waste, 155–156
    disaster prevention measures waste, 159
    large machines waste, 154–155
    materials waste, 157
    parts waste, 157
    searching waste, 154
    shish-kabob production waste, 158
    walking waste, 153–154
    waste in air-processing machines, 156–157
    waste in defective goods production, 159
    waste in meetings, 158
    watching waste, 154
    workpiece motion waste, 158–159
5S approach, xii, 230, 237–238, 455, 689, 721
    as bridge to other improvements, 264
    as prerequisite for flow production, 344
    benefits, 238–243
    changeover 5S checklist, 512
    for factory improvement, 15–17
    in changeover procedure improvement, 502
    keys to success, 262–264
    meaning, 243–249, 250
    orderliness applied to jigs and tools, 307–319
    red tag strategy for visual control, 268–293
    red tags and signboards, 265–268
    role in changeover improvement, 533
    seiketsu (cleaned up), 246–247
    seiri (proper arrangement), 243–245
    seiso (cleanliness), 246
    seiton (orderliness), 245–246
    shitsuke (discipline), 247–249
    signboard strategy for visual orderliness,
        293–306
    visible 5Ss, 249–262
5S badges, 255, 257

5S checklists, 258, 259
    for changeover, 818–819
5S contests, 258
5S implementation memo, case study, 286
5S maps, 261–262
5S memos, 755–757
5S mini motto boards, 255, 257
5S patrol score sheet, 258–259, 260
5S photo exhibit, 260
5S radar chart, 754
5S stickers, 257, 258
5S-related forms, 747
    5S checklists for factories, 747–749
    5S checklists for offices, 753
    5S checklists for workshops, 750–752
    5S memos, 755–757
    5S radar chart, 764
    cleaning checklist, 768–770
    display boards, 775–776
    five-point checklist to assess cleaned-up
        status, 771–774
    lists of unneeded inventory and equipment,
        764–767
    red tag campaign reports, 761–763
    red tags, 758–760
5W1H Sheet, 131, 744–746
    and on-site experience, 233, 235
    first Why guidelines, 233
    follow-up after line stops, 234
    three 5W1H essentials, 233
    waste prevention with, 232–233
7 Ms plus E&I, 551, 552

A

A-B control, 676, 677
Acceptable Quality Level (AQL), 121, 122

Accident-prevention devices, 698
    poka-yoke, 699–709
Accidents
    plywood gluing process, 696
    reasons for, 685–687
Actual work environment. *See* On-site
    experience
Added-value work, 75
Address signboards, 299
Adjustment errors, 560
Adjustment waste, 510
Administrative waste, 173
    and clerical standardization, 229
    disposal case study, 291
After-sales service part requests, 162
Air-processing machines, waste in, 156–157
Airplane *andon,* 466
Alerts, 672
Aluminum casting deburring operation,
    operations analysis table, 192
Amplifier-equipped proximity switches, 578
Andon systems, xiii, 11, 129, 231, 676, 679,
    680, 682
    hire method for using, 465–466
    illuminating factory problems with, 464
    operation *andon,* 468–469
    paging *andon,* 465–466
    progress *andon,* 469–470
    types of, 465
    warning *andon,* 466–468
    waste prevention using, 232
Anticipatory buying, 162
Anticipatory large lot production, 286–287
Anticipatory manufacturing, 162
Apparent minor defects, 680
Appropriate inventory, 96
Arm motions, 220–221
Arrow diagrams, 187–188, 211, 347, 730
    applications, 730
    examples, 731–732
    printed circuit board assembly shop, 189
    tutorial, 187–190
ASEAN countries, xi
Assembly line
    applying *jidoka* to, 660
    extending *jidoka* to, 676–682
    jidoka o prevent oversights in parts
        assembly, 680–681
    stopping at preset position, 69, 678–680
Assembly method error, 678
Assembly parts, exchange of, 499

Assembly processes
    changeover example, 495
    changing to meet client needs, 20
    establishing specialized lines for, 371–373
    kanban in, 447–448, 448
    management of, 81
    manpower reduction example, 428
    multi-process operations in, 363
    standing while working in, 355–359
    warning *andon* for long, 468
    warning *andon* for short, 467
Assembly step omission, 592
Attitude adjustment, 143–144
Auditory control, 120, 231
    waste prevention with, 230–232
Auto feed time, 635
Auto parts machining line, 400
Auto-extract devices, 657
Auto-input devices, 657
Automatic shut-off, 672
Automation, 102–103, 111
    limitations of, 79
    reinforcement of waste by, 111
    vs. Jidoka (human automation), 656,
        657–658
Automobile assembly plant, parts shelves,
    460, 461
Awareness revolution, 103, 104, 105, 159,
    176, 199, 344, 641, 721
    as premise for JIT production, 46, 344
    as prerequisite for factory improvement,
        13–15

B

Back-door approach, to waste discovery,
    181–183
Back-to-the-source inspection, 168, 170–172
Backsliding, 229
Basic Spirit principles, 203, 204
Baton touch zone method, 359, 368, 491, 492
Bills of materials, 81, 83
Blade exchange, 498
Board insertion errors, 594
Body movement principles, 220–221, 220–223
Body, as main perceptive instrument, 134
Bolt removal, eliminating need for, 521, 536
Bolt tightening reductions, 520
Boltless approach, 535

Boltless die exchange, 523
Bolts
    as enemies, 509, 535
    making shorter, 535
Bottlenecked processes, 364
Bottom-up improvements, 134–139
Bracket attachment errors, 603
Brainstorming, 208
    factory problems as opportunities for, 208
Breakdowns
    for standard operations charts, 638
    reducing through 5Ss, 241
Bridge defects, 598
Brush omission errors, 609
Buyer's market, 18
Bypass method, as leveling technique, 491–492

C

Capacity imbalances, 161–162
    between processes, 214–215
    overcoming through 5Ss, 239
    retention and, 161–162
Capacity leveling, 21
Capacity requirements planning (CRP), 442
Capacity utilization rates, 68, 331, 341, 684
    and variety of product models, 504
Capacity-load imbalances, 151
Capital procurement, 93
Caravan style operations, 407, 423
Case studies
    drilling machine worker separation, 669–672
    factory revolution, 287–289
    red tag strategy at Company S, 285–289
Cash-convertible assets, 93
Caster strategy, 349–350, 420. *See also* Movable machines
Chair-free operations, 19
Change, resistance to, 40, 201
Changeover 5S checklist, 512
Changeover costs, 73
    component costs, 73, 74
    variation in, 597
Changeover improvement list, 505, 810–811
    time graph analysis, 513

Changeover improvement procedures, 500–502
    applying 5Ss to eliminate waste, 502
    changeover improvement list, 505
    changeover *kaizen* teams for, 503–506
    changeover operations analysis, 501–502, 506–508
    changeover operations analysis charge, 508
    changeover results table, 507
    eliminating waste with 5Ss, 508–511
    external changeover procedures, 501
    identifying wasteful operations, 508–511
    improving external changeover, 502
    improving internal changeover, 502
    injection molding process case study, 515–517
    internal changeover procedures, 500
    kaizen team, 501
    public changeover timetable, 505
    transforming internal changeover to external changeover, 502
    waste, 501
Changeover improvement rules, 532–533
    role of 5Ss, 533–534
Changeover *kaizen* teams, 501, 503–506
Changeover operations, 71, 347, 723
    adjustment waste in, 510
    and introduction of synchronization, 373
    approach to changeover times, 499–500
    assembly line improvement example, 495
    avoidance of, and retention, 162
    balancing costs with inventory maintenance costs, 72
    changing standard parameters, 499
    exchange of dies and blades, 498
    exchanging assembly parts, 499
    external changeover time, 500
    general set-up, 499
    in JIT production system, 11
    internal changeover time, 500
    minimizing number, 216
    procedures for improvement, 500–532
    production leveling strategies for, 494–495
    rationale for improvement, 497–498
    reducing through 5Ss, 242
    replacement waste in, 509–510
    seven rules for improving, 532–539
    shortening time for, 494
    standardizing, 538–539
    time-consuming nature of, 216, 219

types of, 498–499
within cycle time, 514
Changeover operations analysis, 501–502,
506–508, 535
chart, 508
Changeover results table, 507, 815–817
Changeover standards, standardizing, 537
Changeover times, 499–500
Changeover work procedure analysis charts,
812–814
Checking, 691
Cleaned up checklist, detail, 256
Cleaned up, visibly, 253
Cleaning checklist, 768–770
Cleanliness, 16, 246, 690–691
five-point checklist, 772
of machinery, 119
visible, 253
Cleanliness check cards, 692
Cleanliness control board, 691
Cleanliness inspection checklist, 254, 690,
692
Cleanliness, Checking, and Oiling (CCO),
689–693
training in, 708
Cleanup, 16, 246–247
Cleanup waste, in external changeover
procedures, 511
Clerical standardization, 229
Client needs, as determinant of capacity, 22
Client orders, as basis for cycle time/pitch, 70
Color coding, 253
for maintenance, 693
for oil containers, 319
in changeover improvements, 534
in *kaizen* boards, 462
Color mark sensors, 574, 580
applications, 582
Combination charts, 224
clarifying human work *vs.* machine work
with, 664
for standard operations, 223–226
steps in creating, 630–632
wood products manufacturer example,
226, 227
Communication
about 5S approach, 263
errors in, and defects, 555–556, 558
Compact equipment, 19, 117–118, 340–341,
427, 484
as condition for flow production,
340–341, 342

building flexibility through, 419
compact shotblaster, 354
compact washing unit, 356
cost savings from, 354
diecast factory case study, 375–376, 377
for multi-process operations, 398–399
separating human and machine work
with, 431
Company cop-out, 107, 108
Company-wide efficiency, 68
Company-wide involvement, with 5S
approach, 262
Complexity
and waste, 648
in moving parts, 694
Component efficiency, 66
Computer-based management, 81
Computerization
and waste, 83
expendable material created by, 157
waste-making, 81
Computers
failure to shorten physical lead-time, 5
red tagging, 278–281
Confirmed production schedule, 439
Constant demand, products *vs.* parts, 475–476
Contact devices, 570
differential transformers, 572
limit switches, 570
microswitches, 570
Container organization, for deliveries, 385
Continuous flow production time, 19
Continuous improvement, 211
Control devices, 567
Control standardization, 228
Control/management waste, 149
Conveyance liveliness index, 304
Conveyance waste, 69, 149, 163–166, 173,
176, 180, 187, 336, 355–356, 392
links to retention, 164
Conveyor systems
appropriate use of, 70–71
improving equipment layout to eliminate,
79
waste hidden in, 67
Conveyor use index, 137
Conveyor waste, 155–156
Cooperative operation confirmation chart,
788–790
Cooperative operations, 367–371, 419
improvement steps for, 369
labor cost reduction through, 427–430

placing parts in front of workers for, 370
 VCR assembly line example, 429
Cooperative operations zones, 370–371
Coordinated work, waste in, 67
Corporate balance sheet, inventory in, 94
Corporate culture, 15
Corporate survival, xii
Corrective maintenance, 688
Cost reduction, 69–71
 and effort invested, 71–74
 and profit, 36
 resistance arguments, 200–201
 through 5Ss, 239
 through *jidoka,* 659
Cost, in PQCDS approach, 3
Cost-up method, 35
Countable products, 119
Craft unions, *vs.* enterprise unions, 393–394
Crane operations, safety *poka-yoke,* 706
Cube improvements, 27
Current assets, 93
Current conditions, analysis to discover
 waste, 185–198
Current liabilities, 94
Current operating conditions, 24
Customer complaints, *vs.* defects, 547–548
Customer lead-time, 99
Customer needs, loss of concern for, 113–114
Customers, role in efficiency improvement,
 62–65
Cutting tools
 layout, 317
 orderliness applied to, 316–319
 placement, 317
 storage, 318
 types of, 317
Cycle list method, 487–489
 reserved seats and, 489–490
Cycle tables, 485
Cycle time, 19, 22, 332, 337, 363, 433, 630,
 634, 637, 647. *See also* Pitch
 and production leveling, 421–422
 and standard operations, 625
 as leveling technique, 485–487
 calculating, 487
 completing operations within, 636
 factors determining, 70
 for standard operations charts, 637
 overproduction and, 677
 smaller equipment for maintaining, 398
 vs. speed, 116

D

Deburring omissions, 589
Defect identification, 546
 and causes of defects, 558–561
 and factors behind defects, 550–558
 defects as people-made catastrophes,
 546–547
 inspection misunderstandings, 547–550
Defect prevention, 168, 177
 assembly step omission, 592
 board insertion errors, 594
 bracket attachment errors, 603
 bridge defects, 598
 brush omission errors, 609
 deburring omissions, 589
 defective-nondefective part mixing errors,
 613
 drilling defects, 600, 675–676
 E-ring omission errors, 611
 equipment improvements for, 640
 gear assembly errors, 614
 grinding process omission, 591
 hole count errors, 588
 hole drilling omission, 593
 hose cut length variations, 597
 incorrect drill position, 601
 left-right attachment errors, 615
 mold burr defects, 674–675
 nameplate omission errors, 608
 packing omission errors, 610
 part omission errors, 607
 pin dimension errors, 595
 press die alignment errors, 596
 product set-up errors, 602
 spindle hole punch process omission, 590
 tap processing errors, 606
 tapping operations, 673–674
 through 5Ss, 241
 through automatic machine detection, 403
 through *jidoka*
 through simplified production operations,
 549
 torque tightening errors, 599
 with *kanban,* 441–442
 with multi-process operations, 392
 workpiece direction errors, 605
 workpiece positioning errors, 605
 wrong part assembly errors, 612
Defect production waste, 176–177, 180

Defect reduction, 168, 544
    with compact machinery, 399
Defect signals, 567
Defect-prevention devices, 659, 669, 673
Defective assembly parts, 678
Defective item display, 457, 458
Defective products
    and inventory, 92
    counting, 119
    ending downstream processing of,
        544–545
    factories shipping, 542
    increases with shish-kabob production,
        158
    increasing inspectors to avoid, 542–544
    inventory and, 90–91
    noncreation of, 545–546
    waste in making, 159
Defective/nondefective part mixing errors,
    613
Defects
    and communication errors, 555–556, 557,
        558
    and inspection, 548
    and production method errors, 555, 557
    and surplus products, 549
    as human-caused catastrophes, 546–547
    causes, 558–561
    due to human errors, 551, 553, 557, 558
    due to machine errors, 554–555, 557
    factors behind, 550–558
    in materials, 553–554, 557
    relationship with errors and inspection,
        543
    stoppages for, 567
    ten worst causes, 561
    vs. customer complaints, 547–548
Delays, reducing through 5Ss, 242
Delivery
    and loading methods, 379
    and transport routes, 380–382
    and visible organization of containers, 385
    applying flow concept to, 378–382
    color coding strategy, 384
    FIFO strategy, 384–385
    frequency of, 380
    in PQCDS approach, 3
    self-management by delivery companies,
        383
Delivery company evaluation table, 382,
    791–793
Delivery schedules, shortening of, 2

Delivery sites
    applying flow concepts to, 382–385
    establishment of, 383
    product-specific, 384
Detach movement, automation of, 671–672,
    673
Deterioration, 686
    and accidents, 685
    preventive measures, 688
    reversing, 688
Die exchange, 498
    improvement for boltless, 523
    minimizing, 497
Die height standardization, 526–527
Die storage sites, proper arrangement and
    orderliness applied to, 530–531
Diecast deburring line, 351
Diecast factory, flow production case study,
    373–378
Differential transformers, 572
Dimensional tolerances, 686
Dimensions, enlarging, 311
Disaster prevention measures, waste in, 159
Discipline, 16, 247–249
    JIT Improvements as, 130
    visible, 254–255
Displacement sensors, 574
    applications, 579–580
Display boards, 775–776
Distribution, applying JIT to, 47
Diversification, 2, 117, 415, 416
    of consumer needs, 62
    through 5Ss, 242
Do it now attitude, 236
Doing, as heart of JIT improvement, 133
Dot it now attitude, 236
Double-feed sensors, 576
    applications, 584
Downstream process control inspection
    method, 169, 170
Drill bit replacement, external changeover
    improvement, 532, 533
Drill bit storage method, improvements, 235
Drill operation, before improvement, 670
Drill position errors, 601
Drilling defects, 600
    avoiding downstream passing of, 675–676
Drilling machine, 662
    detach movement, 671–672
    hold motion automation, 671
    jidoka case study, 669–672

safety plate for, 703, 704
separating human from machine work on, 402

E

E-ring omission errors, 611
Economical lot sizes, 72
Economy of motion, 642
Economy of scale, 45
Efficiency
    and production leveling, 69
    approaches to, 59–61
    customer as driver of, 62
    estimated *vs.* true, 59–61
    individual and overall, 66–69
    maximizing at specific processes, 484
    overall, 484, 492
    raising in individual processes, 68
    shish-kabob *vs.* level production
        approaches, 484, 486
Electric screwdrivers, combining, 315
Emergency *andon*, 464
Employees, as basic asset, 108
End-of-month rush, 162
Energy waste
    due to inventory, 325
    through inventory, 91
Engineering technologies, applying JIT
        improvement to, 334
Engineering-related forms, 777
    5S checklist for changeover, 818–819
    changeover improvement lists, 810–811
    changeover results tables, 815–817
    changeover work procedure analysis
        charts, 812–814
    cooperative operation confirmation chart,
        788–790
    delivery company evaluation charts,
        791–793
    JIT delivery efficiency list, 794–796
    line balance analysis charts, 785–787
    model and operating rate trend charts,
        805–807
    multiple skills evaluation chart, 799–801
    multiple skills training schedule, 797–798
    P-Q analysis lists/charts, 777–781
    parts-production capacity work table,
        822–824

poka-yoke/zero defects checklist,
        820–821
    process route diagrams, 782
    production management boards, 802–804
    public changeover timetables, 808–809
    standard operations combination chart,
        825–826
    standard operations form, 831–833
    summary table of standard operations,
        827–828
    work methods table, 829–830
Enterprise unions, *vs.* craft unionis, 393–394
Enthusiasm, as prerequisite for innovation,
        143, 144
Equal-sign manufacturing cells, 362
Equipment
    applying *jidoka* to, 660
    automation and human automation,
        102–103
    compact, 19, 117–118
    ease of maintenance, 119
    ease of operation, 118
    ergonomics recommendations, 222
    for flow production, 389
    improvements facilitating standard
        operations, 640
    modification for multi-process operations,
        406
    movability, 64–65, 117–118
    obtaining information from, 119–120
    shish-kabob *vs.* flow production
        approaches, 331
    standardization in Japanese factories, 395
    versatility and specialization, 116–117
    vs. work operations improvements,
        103–108
Equipment breakdown, 708
    acceptance of, 683
    apparent minor defects, 680
    below-expectation performance, 686
    breakdown stage, 686
    intermittent stoppage stage, 686
    latent minor defects stage, 680
    preventing, 693–695
    stages, 685, 687
Equipment constitution, 694
Equipment costs
    and *jidoka*, 666
    vs. labor costs, 658
Equipment improvement, 103, 104, 106
    and company cop-out, 108
    based on manufacturing flow, 114–120

cost of, 104, 109–111
irreversibility of, 112, 113–114
not spending money on, 207–208
reinforcement of waste by, 111–112
twelve conditions for, 114–120
typical problems, 108–114
Equipment improvement problems, 110
Equipment layout
   applying *jidoka* to, 662
   as condition for flow production, 336–337, 342
   for flow production, 389
   in order of processing, 353–355
   shish-kabob *vs.* flow production approaches, 330
Equipment signboards, 295
Equipment simplification, 400
Equipment waste, 149
Error control, 567
Error prevention boards, 457, 458
Errors, relationships with defects and inspection, 543
Estimate-based leveling, 23
Estimated efficiency, 59–61
Estimated lead-time, 98–99
Estimated production schedule, 439
Estimated quality, 122
Excess capacity, 174
Excuses, 202, 205
Expensive improvements, failure of, 206
Experiential wisdom, 210–211
External changeover improvements, 529–532
   carts reserved for changeover, 531–532
   drill bit replacement example, 532
   proper arrangement and orderliness in die storage sites, 530–531
External changeover procedures, 501
   cleanup waste in, 511
   improving, 502
   preparation waste in, 510
   waste in, 510–511
External changeover time, 500

F

Factory
   as best teacher of improvements, 134–139
   as living organism, 230
Factory bath, 270

Factory graveyards, 73
Factory improvement
   5Ss for, 15–17
   awareness revolution prerequisite, 13–15
   shortening physical lead-times through, 6
   vs. JIT improvements, 13
Factory layout diagram, 188
Factory myths
   anti-JIT production arguments, 40–44
   fixed ideas and JIT production approach, 44–47
   sales price/cost/profit relations, 35–40
Factory problems, 326
   as brainstorming opportunity, 208
   illuminating with *andon,* 464
   stopgap responses to, 150
   ubiquitousness of, 251
Factory revolution, 287–289
Factory-based innovation, xiii, 133
Factory-wide efficiency, 68
Feed motion, 664
   applying *jidoka* to, 665
   jidoka, 670, 671
Feet, effective use of, 221–222, 223
Fiber optic switches, 575, 579
Finance, inventory and, 92–95
Fine-tuning waste, 537
   removal, 523–527
Fingernail clipping debris, device preventing, 247
First-in/First-Out (FIFO), 302–303, 461, 462
   as delivery strategy, 384–385
Five levels of quality assurance achievement, 542–546
Five whys, 24, 130–134, 183, 184, 210, 236
   applying to changeover improvements, 535
   waste discovery through, 208–210
Five-point checklist, 771
   for cleanliness, 772
   for proper arrangement, 772
Five-point cleaned up checklist, 255, 257–258, 773, 774
Fixed ideas, 235
   about conveyors, 156
   avoiding for waste prevention, 235–236
   direct challenge to, 43
   eliminating for waste removal, 204
   kanban, 447
   large lot production, 417
   wall of, 210
Fixed liabilities, 94

Flexibility
   in baton touch zone method, 491
   mental origins of, 420
Flexible production, 419
Flexible staff assignment system, 63, 65, 417, 419
Flow analysis, 188
   summary chart, 189, 190
Flow components, 56
Flow control, 567
Flow devices, 108, 109
Flow manufacturing, xii, 9–10, 49, 64, 70, 79–84. *See also* One-piece flow
   and line improvements, 25
   making waste visible by, 17
   role in JIT introduction, 17–19
   seven requirements, 19
Flow of goods, 159–160, 641, 646
   device improvements facilitating, 638–640
Flow production, 50, 321, 564–565
   and evils of inventory, 324–328
   and inventory accumulation, 321–324
   applying to delivery sites, 382–385
   approach to processing, 329–330
   at diecast factory, 374, 376
   between factories, 332–333, 378–385
   caster strategy, 349–350
   defect prevention with, 721
   diecast factory case study, 373–378
   eight conditions for, 333–341
   equipment approach, 331
   equipment layout in, 330
   for production leveling, 492–494
   in medical equipment industry, 423
   in multi-process operations, 388
   in-process inventory approach, 331
   interrelationship of factors, 343
   lead time approach, 331
   operator approaches, 330–331
   preparation for, 344–350
   procedure for, 350–373
   rational production approach in, 330
   reducing labor cost through, 422–424
   sink cabinet factory example, 493
   steps in introducing, 343–373
   straight-line method, 340
   U-shaped manufacturing cell method, 340
   vs. shish-kabob production, 328–332
   waste elimination techniques, 341–342
   within-factory, 332–333, 333–341
Flow shop layout, 395
Flow unit improvement, 639

Forms, 711–714
   5S-related, 747–776
   engineering-related, 777–833
   for standard operations, 626–628
   JIT introduction-related, 834–850
   overall management, 716–729
   waste-related, 730–746
Free-floating assembly line, 356, 357
Full lot inspection, 120–122
Full parallel operations, 225
Full work system, 175, 365, 676–677
   A-B control, 677
   devices enabling, 368
   pull production using, 367
Function-specific inventory management, 305

G

Gear assembly errors, 614
General flow analysis charts, 733–734
General purpose machines, 331, 340
Golf ball *kanban* systems, 450–451
Graph time, 633
Gravity, *vs.* muscle power, 221
Grinding process omission, 591
Groove processing lifter, separating human/machine work, 649
Group Technology (GT) lines, 347
   for line balancing, 491

H

Hand delivery, 365
Hand-transferred one-piece flow, 337, 338
   pull production using, 366
Handles/knobs, 223
Hands-on improvements, 9, 140
Height adjustments, avoiding, 538
Hirano, Hiroyuki, xiii
Hold motion, automation of, 671
Hole count errors, 588
Hole drilling omission, 593
Horizontal development, 24–25, 391
Hose cut length variations, 597
Household electronics assembly, labor cost reduction example, 428

Human automation, 12, 62, 102–103, 159, 554, 655. *See also Jidoka* (human automation)
  and removal of processed workpieces, 668
  and setup of unprocessed workpieces/startup, 669
  applying to feeding workpieces, 665
  applying to return to starting positions, 667
  for multi-process operations, 402
Human error waste, 173, 674
  and defect prevention, 551–553
  basic training to prevent, 562–563
  defects and, 546–547
  eliminating by multiple skills training, 563
  minimizing, 177
Human movement
  body movement principles, 220–223
  removing wasteful, 217–223
Human work, 658
  clarifying with combination charts, 664
  compact PCB washer example, 431
  procedure for separating from machines, 682–689
  separating from machine work, 64, 118, 400–402, 406, 430–432, 640, 649–650, 660–662, 702, 703
Humanity, coexistence with productivity, 387–388

I

Idle time waste, 66, 67, 69, 156, 173, 178–179, 180, 682
  cooperative operations as solution to, 367–371
Impact wrench, 680, 681
Implementation, 139–144
  of multi-process operations, 405
Implementation rate, for waste removal, 205–206
Improvement
  and enthusiasm, 143, 144
  intensive, 266–268
  making immediate, 538
  poor man's approach, 106
  spending on, 284

  spirit of, 43
  with visual control systems, 453–454
Improvement days, weekly, 32
Improvement goals, 191
Improvement lists, 33–34
Improvement meetings, 32–33, 33
Improvement promotion office, 31–32
Improvement results chart, 462, 844–845
Improvement teams, 31, 32
Improvements
  bottom-up *vs.* top-down, 134–139
  factory as best teacher, 134–139
  implementing, 24
  mental *vs.* physical, 130–134
  passion for, 143–144
  promoting, 126–130
  pseudo, 126–130
Improving actions, 220
In Time concept, 48
In-factory *kanban,* 443, 444–445
In-line layout, 364, 376
  compact shotblaster for, 377
  washing units, 365
In-process inventory, 101, 102, 161, 175, 447, 484
  and standard operations, 625–626
  for standard operations charts, 637
  production *kanban* for, 445
  reduction of, 647, 649
  relationship to *kanban,* 435
  shish-kabob *vs.* flow production approaches, 331
  symbols for standard operations charts, 637
Inconsistency, 152, 643
  eliminating, 151
Independent improvement, 688–689
Independent maintenance, 688–689
Independent process production, 53
  inflexibility in, 54
Independent quality control inspection method, 169, 170
Individual efficiency, 66–69
Industrial engineering (IE), xii
  and conveyor use index, 137
  motion study in, 642
  vs. JIT method, 136
Industrial fundamentalism, 105, 106
Industrial robots, 668
Inexpensive machines, versatility of, 117
Information inspection, 168, 169
Inherent waste, 79–84

Injection molding process
 burr defect prevention, 674
 internal changeover improvement case
  study, 515–517
Injuries
 reasons for, 695–697
 reducing through 5Ss, 241
Innovation, 13, 37
 and JIT production, 47–49
 enthusiasm as prerequisite for, 143
 factory-based, xiii
 in JIT production, 47–49
 JIT production as, 27
Inspection, 56, 160, 187
 back-to-the-source inspection, 170–172
 eliminating need through *jidoka,* 674
 failure to add value, 168
 failure to eliminate defects, 120
 increasing to avoid defective products,
  542–544
 information inspection, 169
 preventive, 564
 relationship to defects, 543, 547–550
 sorting inspection, 169
Inspection buzzers, waste prevention with,
 232
Inspection functions
 building into JIT system, 119
 full lot inspection, 120–122
 sampling inspection, 120–122
Inspection waste, 149
Inspection-related waste, 167–168
Integrated tool functions, 223
Intensive improvement, 266–268
 timing, 268
Interest payment burden, 324, 326
 inventory and, 90
Intermittent stoppage stage, in equipment
 breakdown, 686
Internal changeover improvements, 518,
 534–535
 bolt tightening reductions, 520
 boltless die exchange, 523
 die height standardization, 526–527
 eliminating need to remove bolts, 521
 eliminating nuts and washers, 521
 eliminating replacement waste, 518–523
 eliminating serial operations, 527–529
 establishing parallel operations, 528
 one-touch tool bit exchange, 522
 protruding jigs *vs.* manual position
  setting, 524

 removing fine-tuning waste, 523–527
 spacer blocks and need for manual dial
  positioning, 526
 spacer blocks and need for manual
  positioning, 524–525
 tool elimination, 519–520
Internal changeover procedures
 changing to external changeover, 511–518,
  534
 improving, 500, 502
 PCB assembly plant case study, 513–514
 transforming to external, 502
 turning into external changeover, 511–518
 waste in, 509–510
 wire harness molding process case study,
  517–518
Internal changeover time, 500
Inventory
 advance procurement requirements, 325
 and conveyance needs, 90
 and defects, 90–91, 92
 and energy waste, 91
 and finance, 92–95
 and interest-payment burden, 90
 and lead-time, 87–89, 88
 and losses due to hoarded surpluses, 325
 and materials/parts stocks, 91
 and price cutting losses, 325
 and ROI, 95
 and unnecessary management costs, 91
 and waste, 48
 as cause of wasteful operations, 325
 as evasion of problems, 176
 as false buffer, 95, 101
 as JIT consultant's best teacher, 89
 as opium of factory, 92–95
 as poor investment, 95–98
 breakdown by type, 161
 concealment of factory problems by, 91,
  92, 326, 327
 evasion of problems with, 163
 evils of, 90–92, 324–328
 FIFO storage method, 303
 in corporate balance sheet, 94
 incursion of maintenance costs by, 325
 interest payment burden due to, 324
 management requirements, 325
 product, in-process, materials, 101, 102
 red tagging, 281–282
 reducing with once-a-day production
  scheduling, 480–481

shish-kabob *vs.* level production
  approaches, 484–485
space waste through, 90, 325
unbalanced, 161
wasteful energy consumption due to, 325
with shish-kabob production, 158
zero-based, 98–102
Inventory accumulation
  and caravan operations, 322
  and changeover resistance, 322
  and distribution waits, 322
  and end-of-month rushes, 323
  and faulty production scheduling, 323
  and just-in-case inventory, 323
  and obsolete inventory flow, 321
  and operator delays, 322
  and resistance to change, 322
  and seasonal adjustments, 323–324
  and standards revision, 323
  and unbalanced capacity, 322
  multiple-process sources of, 322
  reasons for, 321
Inventory assets, 715
Inventory control, 126
Inventory flow, obsolete, 321
Inventory graveyard, 324
Inventory liveliness index, 303–304
Inventory maintenance costs, 72
Inventory management
  function-specific method, 305
  product-specific method, 305
  with *kanban,* 436
Inventory reduction, 87, 89, 125
  case study, 288, 289, 377
Inventory stacks, 303
Inventory waste, 175–176, 180
Irrationality, 152, 643
  eliminating, 151
Item characteristics method, 568, 569
Item names, for signboards, 299–300
Ivory tower syndrome, 22

J

Japanese industrial structure, 1980s
  transformation of, xi
Jidoka (human automation), 12, 62, 102–103,
  103–108, 655, 724
  applying to feeding workpieces, 665

automation *vs.,* 656, 657–658
cost considerations, 667, 669
defect prevention through, 672–676
detach movement, 671–672
drilling machine case study, 669–672
extension to assembly line, 676–682
feed motion, 670
full work system, 676–677
manual labor *vs.,* 655, 656
mechanization *vs.,* 656
preventing oversights in nameplate
  attachments, 681–682
steps toward, 655–657
three functions, 658–660
Jigs
  5-point check for orderliness, 256
  applying orderliness to, 307
  color-coded orderliness, 368–369
  combining, 314
  easy-to-maintain orderliness for, 307
  eliminating through orderliness strategies,
    313–316
  indicators for, 308
  outlined orderliness, 309
JIT delivery efficiency list, 794–796
JIT improvement cycle, 144
  roles of visual control tools in, 473
JIT improvement items, 837–840
JIT improvement memo, 836
JIT improvements, 12, 13
  "doing" as heart of, 133
  and changeover costs, 74
  and parts list depth, 82
  as discipline, 130
  as religion, 138
  as top-down improvement method, 135
  basis in ideals, 12
  case study, 288
  cube improvements, 27
  factory as true location of, 34
  from within, 139–143
  hostile environment in U.S. and Europe,
    107
  improvement lists, 33–34
  improvement meetings, 32–33
  improvement promotion office, 31–32
  lack of faith in, 41
  line improvements, 25–26
  plane improvements, 26–27
  point improvements, 25
  promoting and carrying out, 30–34
  requirement of faith, 139

sequence for introducing, 21
seven stages in acceptance of, 140–144
ten arguments against, 299
vs. JIT production management, 7
vs. labor intensification, 86
weekly improvement days for, 32
JIT innovation, 13
JIT introduction steps, 12–13
   5Ss for factory improvement, 15–17
   awareness revolution step, 13–15
   department chiefs' duties, 28–29, 30
   division chiefs' duties, 28
   equipment operators" duties, 30
   factory superintendents' duties, 28–29
   flow manufacturing, 17–19
   foremens' duties, 30
   leveling, 20–22
   president's duties, 28
   section chiefs' duties, 30
   standard operations, 23–24
JIT introduction-related forms, 834
   improvement memo, 836
   improvement results chart, 844–845
   JIT leader's report, 849–850
   JIT Ten Commandments, 834–835
   list of JIT improvement items, 837–840
   weekly report on JIT improvements,
      846–848
JIT leader's report, 849–850
JIT Management Diagnostic List, 715–718
JIT production
   adopting external trappings of, 472
   as new field of industrial engineering, xii
   company-wide promotion, 28, 29
   elimination of waste through, xi
   five stages of, 719, 721, 726, 728
   guidance, education and training in, 30
   hands-on experience, 30
   in-house seminar, 343
   innovation in, 47–49
   linked technologies in, 334
   promotional organization, 31
   radar chart, 727
   setting goals for, 28
   structure, 720
JIT production management
   distinguishing from JIT improvements, 7
   vs. conventional production management,
      1–3
JIT production system
   as total elimination of waste, 145
   changeover, 11

flow manufacturing, 9–10
from vertical to horizontal development,
   24–27
human automation, 12
introduction procedure, 12–14
jidoka, 12
kanban system, 10
leveling, 11
maintenance and safety, 12
manpower reduction, 10
multi-process handling, 10
organizing for introduction of, 27–30
overview, 7–9
quality assurance, 11
standard operations, 11–12
steps in establishing, 14
view of waste, 152
visual control, 10–11
JIT radar charts, 719, 727, 729
JIT study groups, 15
JIT Ten Commandments, 834–835
Job shop layout, 395
Just-in-case inventory, 323
Just-In-Time
   anatomy of, 8–9
   and cost reduction, 69–71
   as consciousness improvement, 139–143
   functions and five stages of development,
      728
   innovation and, 47–49
   view of inspection work, 168

K

Kaizen boards, 462
   visual control and, 471–473
   with improvement results displays, 463
Kanban systems, xii, xiii, 7, 8, 10, 11, 52,
      54, 174, 231, 365, 692, 722
   administration, 447–451
   and defect prevention, 441–442
   and downstream process flow, 441
   and in-process inventory, 435
   applying to oiling, 693
   appropriate use of, 70–71
   as autonomic nervous system for JIT
      production, 440
   as tool for promoting improvements, 441
   as workshop indicators, 442

differences from conventional systems, 435–437
factory improvements through, 440–441
fixed ideas about, 447
functions, 440–441
in processing and assembly lines, 447–448
in-factory *kanban,* 444–445
novel types, 450–451
production *kanban,* 445
production leveling through, 442
purchasing-related, 449–450
quantity required, 445–447
rules, 441–442
signal *kanban,* 445
supplier *kanban,* 443
types of, 442–447
visual control with, 457
vs. conventional production work orders, 437–439
vs. reordering point method, 435–437
waste prevention with, 232

L

L-shaped line production, 360
Labor cost reduction, 415, 418, 722
and elimination of processing islands, 421
and mental flexibility, 420
and movable equipment, 420–421
and multi-process operations, 421
and production leveling, 421–422
and standardized equipment and operations, 421
approach to, 415–418
display board for, 433–434
flow production for, 422–424
multi-process operations for, 424–426
multiple skills training schedule for, 432–433
steps, 419–422
strategies for achieving, 422–432
through cooperative operations, 427–430
through group work, 426–427
through separating human and machine work, 430–432
visible, 432–434
vs. labor reduction, 417–418
Labor cost reduction display board, 433–434

Labor intensity/density, 84–86
vs. production output, 86
Labor per unit, 649
Labor reduction, 63, 418, 647
vs. labor cost reduction, 417–418
vs. worker hour minimization, 66–69
Labor savings, 418
Labor unions, 107. *See also* Craft unions; Enterprise unions
and multi-process operations, 393–394
Labor-intensive assembly processes, 217
Large lot sizes, 18, 62, 73, 278, 321, 398, 483, 598
and changeover times, 216
and machine waste, 155
as basis of production schedules, 476
case study, 286–287
fixed ideas about, 417
switching to small-lot flow from, 639
Large machines waste, 154–155, 331
Large-scale container deliveries, 381
Latent minor defects, 680
Latent waste, 198
Lateral development, 27, 378, 505, 506
Lateral improvement makers, 167
Lathes, 682
three kinds of motion, 663
worker separation from, 702
Layout improvement, 638
Lead-time
and inventory, 88
and lot sizes, 498
and production lot size, 72
and work stoppage, 59–61
estimated *vs.* real, 98–99
inventory and, 87–89
lengthened with shish-kabob production, 158
paper, 4, 5
physical, 5
product, 4
reduction with multi-process operations, 393
shish-kabob *vs.* flow production approaches, 331, 486
shish-kabob *vs.* level production approaches, 484–485
shortening by reducing processing time, 55
Leadership, for multi-process operations, 404–405
Left-right attachment errors, 615

Leg motion, minimizing, 221
Level production, 475, 723. *See also* Leveling
    as market-in approach, 482
    vs. once-a-day production, 481
    vs. shish-kabob production, 482–485, 486
Leveling, 50, 476. *See also* Level production;
    Production leveling
    and production schedule strategies,
      477–482
    approach to, 476–477
    capacity and load, 21
    estimate-based, 23
    reality-based, 23
    role in JIT introduction, 20–22
    role in JIT production system, 11
    techniques, 482–492
Leveling techniques, 485
    baton touch zone method, 491
    bypass method, 491–492
    cycle list method, 487–489
    cycle tables, 485
    cycle time, 485–487
    nonreserved seat method, 487–489
    reserved seat method, 489–490
Limit switches, 403, 470, 570, 676, 677, 706,
    708
Line balance analysis charts, 785–787
Line balancing
    at PCB assembly plant, 514
    SOS system for, 217
    strategies for, 491
Line balancing analysis tables, 358
Line design, based on P-Q analysis, 346, 347
Line efficiency, 68
Line improvements, 25–26
Line stops, 470
    5W1H follow-up after, 234
    at preset positions, 678–680
    with *poka-yoke* devices, 675
Lined up inventory placement, 304–306
Linked technologies, in JIT production, 334
Litter-preventive device, for drill press, 248
Load leveling, 21
Loading methods, 379
Long-term storage, case study, 291
Lot sizes, 45, 87
    and lead time, 72
    large *vs.* small, 71–74
Lot waiting waste, 215–216, 219
    waste removal, 219
Low morale, 16

M

Machine errors
    and defect prevention, 554–555
    poka-yoke to prevent, 564
Machine operating status, *andon*
    notification of, 466
Machine placement, waste and, 185
Machine signboards, 295
Machine standardization, 228
Machine start-up, applying *jidoka* to, 663,
    668
Machine work
    clarifying with combination charts, 664
    compact PCB washer example, 431
    separating from human work, 64, 118,
      400–402, 406, 430–432, 640,
      649–650, 660–662
Machine/people waiting, 214
Machines
    as living things, 120–122
    shish-kabob *vs.* level production
      approaches, 484, 486
    with strong constitution, 708
Machining line, full work system, 677
Maintenance, 683, 725
    and accidents, 685–687
    and possible utilization rate, 684–685
    breakdown prevention, 693–695
    Cleanliness, Checking, and Oiling (CCO)
      approach, 689–693
    defined, 684–689
    existing conditions, 683–684
    full-fledged, 708–709
    improving through 5Ss, 241
    in JIT production system, 12
    of equipment, 119
Maintenance campaigns, 687–689
Maintenance errors, 560
Maintenance prevention, 688
Maintenance technicians, 689
Make-believe automation, 79
Man, material, machine, method, and
    management (5Ms), 152, 153
Management-related forms, 715
    five stages of JIT production, 719, 721–725
    JIT Management Diagnostic List, 715–718
    JIT radar charts, 719
Manpower flexibility, 338
Manpower needs, based on cycle time, 22

Manpower reduction, 10, 62–65, 63, 337, 392
   household electronics assembly line
      example, 428
   improving efficiency through, 61
   through flow production, 422–424
Manual dial positioning, eliminating with
      spacer blocks, 526
Manual labor, 655, 656
Manual operations, two-handed start/stop,
      220
Manual position setting, eliminating need for,
      524
Manual work time, 635
Manual-conveyance assembly lines,
      progress *andon* in, 469
Manufacturing
   as service industry, 1
   five essential elements, 553
   nine basic elements (7Ms plus E&I), 552
   purpose of, 1
Manufacturing flow, as basis for equipment
      improvements, 114–120
Manufacturing process, components, 56
Manufacturing waste, 149
Market demand fluctuations, unsuitability of
      kanban for, 436
Market price, as basis of sales price, 35
Market-in production, xii, 416, 555
   level production as, 482
Marshaling, 306
Mass production equipment, 216, 219
Material handling
   building flexibility into, 419
   minimizing, 176
   vs. conveyance, 164
Material handling costs, 159, 163
Material requirements planning (MRP), 52
Materials flow
   device improvements facilitating, 638–640
   standard operations improvements, 641
Materials inventory, 101, 102
Materials waiting, 215, 218
Materials waste, 157
Materials, and defect prevention, 553–554
Measuring tools
   orderliness for, 318
   types, 319
Mechanization, 656
Medical equipment manufacturing,
      manpower reduction example, 423
Meetings, waste in, 158

Mental improvements
   vs. implementation, 140
   vs. real improvements, 130–134
Metal passage sensors, 574
   applications, 581
Microswitch actuators, 571
Microswitches, 570, 674
Milling machine, safety *poka-yoke* for,
      705–706
Minimum labor cost, 62
Missing item errors, 587, 607–611, 678
Mistake-proofing, 119
Mistakes, correcting immediately, 207
Mixed loads, 379
Mixed-model flow production, 492
Mizusumashi (whirligig beetle), 465
Model and operating rate trend charts,
      805–807
Model lines, analyzing for flow production,
      348
Mold burr defects, prevention, 674–675
Monitoring, *vs.* managing, 123–126, 126–130
Motion
   and work, 74–79
   as waste, 76, 78, 79, 84
   costs incurred through, 77
   economy of, 642
   lathes and, 663
   vs. work, 657, 659
Motion study, 642
Motion waste, 639
   improvements with standard operations,
      639
Motor-driven chain, 694
Movable machines, 64–65, 65, 117–118, 165,
      354, 420
   and caster strategy, 349–350
   building flexibility through, 419
Movement
   as waste, 178
   improving operational efficiency, 642–649
   non-added value in, 190
Muda (waste), 643
Multi-process operations, 10, 19, 64, 330,
      359, 362–363, 387–388, 417, 722
   abolishing processing islands for, 396–398
   and labor unions, 393–394
   as condition for flow production, 337–338
   basis for pay raises in, 394
   compact equipment for, 398–399
   effective leadership for, 404–405
   equipment layout for, 389

equipment modification for, 406
factory-wide implementation, 405
human assets, 389
human automation for, 402–403
human work *vs.* machine work in, 400–402
in wood products factory, 425
key points, 395–404
labor cost reduction through, 424–426
multiple skills training for, 400
one-piece flow using, 338
operational procedures for, 389
poka-yoke for, 402–403
precautions, 404–406
promoting perseverance with, 406
questions from western workers, 393–395
safety priorities, 403–404, 406
simplified work procedures for, 404
standard operations improvements, 639
standing while working for, 399–400
training costs for, 394–395
training for, 421
training procedures, 407–413
transparent operations in, 405
U-shaped manufacturing cells for, 395–396
vs. horizontal multi-unit operations,
    388–393
Multi-process workers, 331
  as condition for flow production, 339
  at diecast factory, 377
Multi-skilled workers, 19, 390
  and standard operations, 650–651
  building flexibility through, 419
Multi-unit operations, 338, 391
  vs. multi-process operations, 388–393
Multi-unit process stations, 390
Multiple skills contests, 405
Multiple skills evaluation chart, 799–801
Multiple skills maps, 432
Multiple skills score sheet, 410, 432
Multiple skills training, 425, 651
  defect prevention with, 563
  for multi-process operations, 400
  schedule for, 432–434
Multiple skills training schedule, 797–798
Multiple-skills training, 407
  demonstration by workshop leaders, 412
  during overtime hours, 409
  five-level skills evaluation for, 408
  hands-on practice, 412
  importance of praise, 413
  in U-shaped manufacturing cells, 410
  schedule, 409

team building for, 408
trainer roles, 413
workshop leader roles, 411
Mura (inconsistency), 643
Muri (irrationality), 643
Mutual aid system, 65

N

Nameplate omission errors, 608
  preventing with *jidoka,* 681–682
Needed items, separating from unneeded
    items, 266
Net time, for standard operations charts, 637
Newly Industrialized Economic Societies
    (NIES), xi
Next process is your customer, 51, 54, 132
Non-value-added steps
  as waste, 147, 171
  in inspection, 170
  in retention, 163
Noncontact switches, 572
  color mark sensors, 574
  displacement sensors, 574
  double-feed sensors, 576
  metal passage sensors, 574
  outer diameter/width sensors, 574
  photoelectric switches, 572, 574
  positioning sensors, 574
  proximity switches, 574
  vibration switches, 574
Nondefective products, counting, 119
Nonreserved seat method, 487–489
Nonunion labor, 394
Nuts and washers, eliminating as internal
    changeover improvement, 521

O

Oil containers, color-coded orderliness, 319
Oil, orderliness for, 318–319
Oiling, 691–693
  kanban for, 693
On-site experience, 190
  and 5W1H method, 233, 235
  by supervisors, 230, 233, 235

Once-a-day production scheduling, 480–482

Once-a-month production scheduling, 478–479

Once-a-week production scheduling, 479–480

One how, 24, 128, 130–134, 183

One-piece flow, 19, 64, 115–116, 165, 185, 419, 639. *See also* Flow manufacturing
  as condition for flow production, 335–336
  discovering waste with, 183–185
  hand-transferred, 338
  in multi-process operations, 388
  maintaining to avoid creating waste, 351–353, 353
  revealing waste with, 350–351, 352
  switching to, under current conditions, 184
  using current equipment layout and procedures, 336

One-touch tool bit exchange, 522

Operation *andon,* 464, 468–469

Operation errors, 560

Operation management, 81

Operation method waiting, 215, 218

Operation methods, conditions for flow production, 342

Operation step method, 568, 569

Operation-related waste, 173, 178, 180

Operational combinations, 193

Operational device improvements, 640

Operational rules, standard operations improvements, 639–640

Operations analysis charts, 735–736

Operations analysis table, 190–192, 735, 736
  aluminum casting deburring operation example, 192

Operations balancing, 219

Operations improvements, 103, 104, 105, 217

Operations manuals, 405

Operations standardization, 228

Operations, improving point of, 220

Operators
  conditions for flow production, 342
  diecast factory case study, 377
  maintenance routines, 691
  reducing gaps between, 370
  shish-kabob *vs.* flow production approaches, 330–331

Opportunistic buying, 162

Optical displacement sensors, 578

Oral instructions, avoiding, 556

Order management, 81

Orderliness, 16, 157, 245–246, 510
  applied ti die storage sites, 530–531
  applying to jigs and tools, 307
  beyond signboards, 302–306
  color-coded, 319, 384
  conveyance liveliness index, 304
  easy-to-maintain, 307, 310–313
  eliminating tools and jigs with, 313–316
  for cutting tools, 316–319
  for measuring tools, 318
  for oil, 318–319
  four stages in evolution, 312
  habitual, 302
  inventory liveliness index, 303–304
  just-let-go principle, 313, 314
  lined up inventory placement, 304–306
  made visible through red tags and signboards, 265–268
  obstacles to, 17
  visible, 252–253

Outer diameter/width sensors, 574
  applications, 578

Outlined orderliness, for jigs and tools, 309–310

Outlining technique, waste prevention with, 231

Overall efficiency, 66

Overkill waste, 173

Overload prevention devices, 706

Overproduction waste, 69, 174–175, 180
  beyond cycle time, 677
  preventing with A-B control, 676–677

Overseas production shifts, xi

P

P-Q analysis, 188, 345–346

P-Q analysis lists/charts, 777–781

Packing omission errors, 610

Paging *andon,* 464, 465–466
  hire method for using, 466

Painting process, reserved seat method example, 490

Paper lead-time, 4, 5

Parallel operations, 224–225, 536
  calculations for parts-production capacity work tables, 634

establishing in transfer machine blade
    replacement, 528
full *vs.* partial, 225
Pareto chart, 132, 457
Parking lots, well- and poorly-managed, 300
Parkinson's Law, 126
Part omission errors, 607
Partial parallel operations, 225
    calculations for parts-production capacity
        work tables, 633–634
Parts assembly
    preventing omission of parts tightening,
        681
    preventing oversights with *jidoka,*
        680–681
Parts development, 52
Parts inventories
    demand trends, 475
    strategies for reducing, 475–476
Parts list, depth and production method, 82
Parts placement
    in cooperative operations, 370
    standard operations improvements, 643
Parts tray/box, visible organization, 385
Parts waste, 157
Parts, improvements in picking up, 643–644
Parts-production capacity work table, 626,
        629, 822–824
    serial operations calculations, 633
    steps in creating, 632–634
Pay raises, basis of, 394
PCB assembly plant, internal-external
        changeover improvements, 513–514
People
    as root of production, 104, 107, 108
    training for multi-process operations, 389
Per-day production total, 487
Per-unit time, 633
Performance below expectations, 686
Personnel costs, and manpower strategies, 63
Photoelectric switches, 572, 574, 682
    applications, 572
    object, detection method, and function,
        573
Physical lead-time, 5
Pickup *kanban,* 444
Piecemeal approach, failure of, xiii
Pin dimension errors, 595
Pinch hitters, 407
Pitch, 66, 67, 337, 433, 469. *See also* Cycle time
    adjusting to worker pace, 358–359
    approaches to calculating, 485

factors determining, 70
failure to maintain, 678
hourly, 482
individual differences in, 67
myth of conveyor contribution to, 156
Pitch buzzers, waste prevention with, 232
Pitch per unit, 649
Plane improvements, 26–27
Plywood gluing process, accidents, 696
Pneumatic cylinders
    safety improvement from, 694
    workpiece removal with, 667
Pneumatic switches, 680–681
Point improvements, 25
    line improvements as accumulation of, 26
Poka-yoke, 119, 159, 177, 675, 680, 682.
        See also Safety
    and defect prevention, 566
    approaches, 568–570
    concept and methodology, 565–568
    control devices, 567
    defect prevention with, 564
    detection devices, 570–585
    drilling machine case study, 703
    for crane operations, 706
    for multi-process operations, 402–403
    milling machine example, 705–706
    safety applications, 703–709, 709
    safety cage on press, 704
    safety plate case, 703
    stop devices, 566–567
    warning devices, 567
Poka-yoke case studies, by defect type,
        586–587
Poka-yoke checklists
    three-point evaluation, 619–620
    three-point response, 620–622
    using, 616–622
Poka-yoke detection devices, 570
    applications, 585
    contact devices, 570–572
    noncontact switches, 572–575
Poka-yoke/zero defects checklist, 820–821
Policy-based buying, 162
Position adjustments, avoiding, 537–538
Positioning sensors, 574
    applications, 577
Positive attitude, 204–205
Possible utilization rate, 684–685, 708
Postural ease, 221
Power, inexpensive types, 222
PQCDS approach, 2, 3

Practical line balancing, 357, 358
Preassembly processes, scheduling, 477
Preparation waste, in external changeover
    procedures, 510
Preset stop positions, 680
Press die alignment errors, 596
Press operator, waste example, 77–78
Presses
    safety problems, 702
    worker separation, 703
Preventive inspection, 564
Preventive maintenance, 688, 708
Previous process-dependent production, 54
Price cutting, due to inventory, 325
Printed circuit board assembly shop, 211
    arrow diagrams, 189, 212
Proactive improvement attitude, 54
Problem-solving, *vs.* evasive responses, 150
Process display standing signboards, 462–463
Process improvement models, 166, 167
Process route diagrams, 782–784
Process route tables, 347, 348
Process separation, 216, 219
Process waiting waste, 214, 218
Process, transfer, process, transfer system, 59
Process-and-go production, 55–59, 57, 59
Process-related waste, 177–178
Processing, 56, 160, 187
    lack of time spent in, 58
    shish-kabob *vs.* flow production
        approaches, 329–330
Processing errors, 586
Processing islands
    abolishment of, 396–398
    eliminating, 421, 426–427
Processing omissions, 586, 588–600
Processing sequence
    at diecast factory, 374, 376
    equipment layout by, 336–337, 353–355
Processing time, reducing to shorten
    lead-time, 55
Processing waste, 166–167, 180
Procrastination, 205, 207
Procurement
    applying JIT to, 47
    standardization, 229
Product inventory, 101, 102
    demand trends, 475
    strategies for reducing, 475–476
Product lead-time, 4
Product model changes
    and capacity utilization rates, 504

avoidance of, 162
Product set-up errors, 602
Product-out approach, 36, 416, 483, 555
    once-a-month production scheduling in,
        479
Product-specific delivery sites, 384
Product-specific inventory management, 305
Production
    equipment- *vs.* people-oriented, 112–113
    roots in people, 104, 108
    waste-free, 49
Production analysis, 345–348
Production as music, 29–50, 51–54
    three essential elements, 50
Production factor waste, 159–160
    conveyance and, 163–166
    inspection and, 167–172
    processing and, 166–167
    retention and, 160–163
Production input, 59, 60
Production *kanban,* 443, 445
Production leveling, 21, 421–422, 482.
       See also Leveling
    as prerequisite for efficiency, 71
    flow production development for, 492–494
    importance to efficiency, 69
    kaizen retooling for, 494–495
    strategies for realizing, 492–494
    with *kanban* systems, 442, 445
Production management
    conventional approach, 3–7
    defined, 6
    management system, 6
    physical system, 6
    vs. JIT production management, 1–3
Production management boards, 457,
       470–471, 802–804
Production method
    and defect prevention, 555
    shish-kabob *vs.* level production, 484, 486
Production output, 59, 60
    and in-process inventory, 89
    and volume of orders, 61
    increasing without intensifying labor, 86
Production philosophy, shish-kabob *vs.*
       level production, 483–484, 486
Production planning, 52
Production schedules, 4
    leveling production, 482
    once-a-day production, 480–482
    once-a-month production, 478–479

once-a-week production, 479–480
strategies for creating, 477
Production standards, 623. *See also* Standard
operations
Production techniques, 715
JIT Management Diagnostic List, 718
Production work orders, *vs. kanban* systems,
437–439
Productivity, 59–61
and volume of orders, 61
boosting with safety measures, 701
coexisting with humanity, 387–388
volume-oriented approach to, 415
Productivity equation, 415, 416
Products, in PQCDS approach, 3
Profit
and cost reduction, 36
losses through motion, 77
Profitable factories, 40
anatomy of, 39
Progress *andon,* 464, 469–470
Proper arrangement, 16, 157, 243–245, 510
applied to die storage sites, 530–531
five-point checklist, 772
made visible through red tags and
signboards, 265–268
obstacles to, 17
visible, 251–252
Proximity switches, 574
applications, 576
Pseudo improvements, 126–130
Public changeover timetable, 505, 808–809
Pull production, 10, 26, 51, 52, 54, 70, 438
flow of information and materials in, 53
relationship to goods, 439
using full work system, 367
using hand delivery, 366
vocal, 371, 372
Punching lathe, worker separation, 702
Purchasing-related *kanban,* 449–450
Push production, 10, 26, 51, 419, 438, 439
as obstacle to synchronization, 364–365
flow of information and materials in, 53

Q

QCD (quality, cost, delivery) approach, 2
Quality
estimated, 122

improving through 5Ss, 241
in PQCDS approach, 3
process-by-process, 123–126
Quality assurance, 724
and defect identification, 546–561
and *poka-yoke* system, 565–585
as starting point in building products,
541–542
in JIT production system, 11
JIT five levels of QA achievement, 542–546
poka-yoke defect case studies, 586–615
use of *poka-yoke* and zero defects
checklists, 616–622
zero defects plan, 561–565
Quality check points, for standard
operations charts, 636–638
Quality control inspection method, 169

R

Radar chart, 727
Rational production, 120–121, 122
shish-kabob *vs.* flow production
approaches, 330
Reality-based leveling, 23
Recession-resistant production system, 8
Red tag campaign reports, 761–763
Red tag criteria, setting, 273–274
Red tag episodes, 281
employee involvement, 284
excess pallets, 283
red tag stickers, 283–284
red tagging people, 282
showing no mercy, 284–285
twenty years of inventory, 281–282
twice red tagged, 282
yellow tag flop, 283
Red tag forms, 271
Red tag items list, 765
Red tag list, computer-operated, 280
Red tag strategy, xii, 17, 265–268, 269–270,
455
campaign timing, 268
case study at Company S, 285–289
criteria setting, 273–274
for visual control, 268–269
implementation case study, 290–293
indicating where, what type, how many,
268

main tasks in, 291
making tags, 274–275
overall procedure, 267
project launch, 271, 273
red tag episodes, 281–285
red tagging computers, 278–281
steps, 270–278, 272
tag attachment, 276
target evaluation, 276–278
target identification, 273
understanding, 282
waste prevention with, 231
Red tag strategy checklist, 292
Red tag strategy report form, 293
Red tag targets
evaluating, 276–278
identifying, 273
Red tags, 758, 759, 760
attaching, 276
example, 275
making, 274–275
Reliability, increasing in equipment, 688
Reordering point method, 435–437, 475
Replacement waste, 509–510
eliminating in internal changeover, 518–523
Required volume planning, 52
Research and development, 37
Reserved carts, for changeover, 531–532
Reserved seat method, 489–490
painting process example, 490
Resistance, 42, 43, 199, 201–202
and arguments against JIT improvement, 200
and inventory accumulation, 322
by foremen and equipment operators, 30
from senior management, 15
to change, 41, 84
to multiple-skills training, 407
Responsiveness, 453
Retention, 56, 57, 160, 186, 187
and anticipatory buying, 162
and anticipatory manufacturing, 162
and capacity imbalances, 161–162
in shish-kabob production, 484
process, retention, transfer system, 59
reducing, 59
waste in, 160–163
Retention waste
eliminating, 213–214
lot waiting waste, 215–216
process waiting waste, 214

Retooling time, 633
Retooling volume, 633
Return on investment (ROI), inventory and, 95
Return to start position, 663
applying *jidoka* to, 666, 667
Returning waste, 511
Rhythmic motions, 221
Rules, for safety, 696, 697, 699

S

S-shaped manufacturing cells, 362
Safety, 152, 406, 725
basic training for, 698–699
defined, 698–699
for multi-process operations, 403–404
full-fledged, 70–709
in JIT production system, 12
in PQCDS approach, 3
in standard operations chart, 701
poka-yoke applications, 703–703
standard operations goals, 624
through 5Ss, 241
visual assurance, 707–708
Safety cage, 704
Safety check points, for standard operations charts, 637
Safety improvement, pneumatic cylinders to springs, 694
Safety plate, 703
Safety strategies for zero injuries/accidents, 699–709
Salad oil example, 312
Sales figures
and equipment improvements, 115
impact of seasons and climatic changes on, 97
Sales price, 36
basis in market price, 35
Sampling inspection, 120–122
Screw-fastening operation, waste in, 148
Searching waste, 154
Seasonal adjustments, 323–324
Seiketsu (cleanup), 16, 239, 246–247
Seiri (proper arrangement), 16, 238, 243–245
photo exhibit, 260
Seiso (cleanliness), 16, 239, 246

Seiton (orderliness), 16, 245–246, 328
    photo exhibit, 260
Self-inspection, 392
Senior management
    approval for 5S approach, 262
    ignorance of production principles, 88
    need to believe in JIT, 139
    on-site inspection by, 264
    responsibility for 5S strategy, 263
    role in awareness revolution, 14–15
    role in production system change, 3
    Seniority, as basis of pay raises, 394
Sensor assembly line, multi-process
      operations on, 363
Sequential mixed loads, 379
Serial operations, 224
    calculations for parts-production capacity
      work tables, 633
    eliminating, 527–529
Set-up
    applying human automation to, 669
    pre-manufacturing, 499
    unprocessed workpieces, 663, 667
Set-up errors, 560, 586, 601–606
Seven QC tools, 132, 133
Seven types of waste, 172–174
    conveyance waste, 176
    defect production waste, 176–177
    idle time waste, 178–179
    inventory waste, 175–176
    operation-related waste, 178
    overproduction waste, 174–175
    process-related waste, 177–178
Shared specifications, 419
Shish-kabob production, 10, 17, 18, 20, 46,
      70, 104, 166, 207
    approach to processing, 329–330
    as large-lot production, 423
    as obstacle to synchronization, 371–373
    disadvantages, 158
    equipment approach, 331
    equipment layout in, 330
    in-process inventory approach, 331
    lead time approach, 331
    operator approaches, 330–331
    production scheduling for, 476
    rational production approach in, 330
    vs. flow production, 328–332
    vs. level production, 482–485, 486
    waste in, 158
Shitsuke (discipline), 16, 239, 247–249
Short-delivery scheduling, 379, 497

Shotblaster
    at diecast factory, 375
    compact, 354, 377, 398–399
Shukan (custom), 689
Signal *kanban,* 443, 445, 446
Signboard strategy, 442, 455, 464
    amount indicators, 301–302
    and FIFO, 302–303
    defined, 294–296
    determining locations, 296
    die storage site using, 530
    for delivery site management, 383
    for visual orderliness, 293–294
    habitual orderliness, 302
    indicating item names, 299–300
    indicating locations, 298
    item indicators, 301
    location indicators, 299
    parking lot item indicator examples, 300
    preparing locations, 296–298
    procedure, 297
    signboard examples, 295
    steps, 296–302
Signboards, 43, 44, 265–268
    overall procedure, 267
    waste prevention with, 231
Simplified work procedures, 404
    and defect prevention, 549
Single-process workers, 339, 375, 419
Single-product factories, 71
Single-product load, 379
Sink cabinet factory, flow production
      example, 493
Skin-deep automation, 79
Slow-but-safe approach, 102–103
Small-volume production, xi, 2, 62, 278, 321,
      497
Social waste, 159
Solder printing process, flow of goods
      improvement, 641
Sorting inspection, 168, 169
Spacer blocks
    and manual positioning, 524–525
    eliminating need for manual dial
      positioning with, 526
Speaker cabinet processing operations,
      improvements, 646–647
Special-order production, 2
Specialization
    in Western *vs.* Japanese unions, 393–394
    vs. multi-process operations, 639

Specialized carts, for changeover operations, 532
Specialized lines, 371–373
Specialized machines, cost advantages, 332
Speed, *vs.* cycle time, 116
Spindle hole punch processing omission, 590
Spirit of improvement, 43, 44
Staff reduction, 62, 418
Standard operating processes (SOPs), 23
Standard operation forms, 626
    parts-production capacity work table, 626
    standard operations chart, 627–628, 628
    standard operations combination chart, 626, 627
    standard operations pointers chart, 626–627, 627
    steps in creating, 630–638
    work methods chart, 627
Standard operations, 24, 50, 65, 193–194, 224, 623, 708–709, 724
    and multi-skilled workers, 650–651
    and operation improvements, 638–649
    as endless process, 624
    combination charts for, 223–226
    communicating meaning of, 652
    cost goals, 624
    cycle time and, 625
    defined, 623
    delivery goals, 624
    eliminating walking waste, 645–649
    equipment improvements facilitating, 640
    equipment improvements to prevent defects, 640
    establishing, 628–630, 629–630, 654
    factory-wide establishment, 652
    forms, 626–628
    goals, 624
    implementing for zero injuries/accidents, 699–703
    improvement study groups for, 653
    improvements to flow of goods/materials, 638–640
    in JIT production system, 11–12
    materials flow improvements, 641
    motion waste elimination through, 639
    movement efficiency improvements, 642–643
    multi-process-operations improvements, 639
    need for, 623–624
    obtaining third-party help, 653
    one-handed to two-handed task improvements, 644–645
    operational rules improvements, 639–640
    parts placement improvements, 643
    picking up parts improvements, 643–644
    preserving, 650–654
    quality goals, 624
    rejection of status quo in, 653
    reminder postings, 652
    role in JIT introduction, 23–24
    safety goals, 624, 697
    separating human work from machine work for, 640, 649–650
    sign postings, 652
    spiral of improvement, 629
    standard in-process inventory and, 625–626
    ten commandments for, 651–654
    three basic elements, 625–626
    transparent operations and, 628
    waste prevention through, 226
    wood products manufacturer's combination charts, 227
    work sequence and, 625
    workshop leader skills, 652, 653
Standard operations chart, 627, 628, 629, 631, 637
    safety points, 700, 701
    steps in creating, 630–632, 636–638
Standard operations combination chart, 193, 457, 626, 627, 629, 631, 825–826
    steps in creating, 634–636
Standard operations form, 831–833
Standard operations pointers chart, 626–627, 627
Standard operations summary table, 827–828
Standard parameters, changeover of, 499
Standardization
    of equipment, 421
    waste prevention by, 228–230
Standby-for-lot inventory, 161
Standby-for-processing inventory, 161
Standing signboards, 462–463
Standing while working, 19, 118, 355, 424, 425, 429
    and cooperative operations, 368
    as condition for flow production, 339
    in assembly lines, 355–359
    in multi-process operations, 399–400
    in processing lines, 359–360
    work table adjustments for, 360
Statistical inventory control methods, 475

Statistical method, 570
　poka-yoke, 659
Status quo
　denying, 205
　failure to ensure corporate survival, 15
　reluctance to change, 42
Steady-demand inventories, 476
Stockpiling, 160
Stop devices, 566–567
Stop-and-go production, 55–59, 57
Stopgap measures, 150
Storage, cutting tools, 318
Straight-line flow production, 340, 360
Subcontracting, applying JIT to, 47
Subcontractors, bullying of, 378
Sudden-demand inventories, 476
Suggestion systems, 36
Supplier *kanban,* 443, 444
Supplies management, 81
Surplus production, 323
　and defects, 549
Sweat workers, 74, 75
Symmetrical arm motions, 220–221
Synchronization, 363–364
　as condition for flow production, 337
　bottlenecked process obstacle, 364
　changeover difficulties, 373
　obstacles to, 364–368
　PCB assembly line, 366, 367
　push method as obstacle to, 364–365
　work procedure variations as obstacle to, 367–371

T

Taboo phrases, 202
　Japanese watch manufacturer, 203
Takt time, 368, 469, 482
Tap processing errors, 606
Tapping operations, defect prevention, 673–674
Temporary storage, 160
Three Ms, in standard operations, 623
Three Ps, 432
Three-station arrangements, 165
Time graph analysis, changeover improvements, 513
Time workers, 75
Tool bit exchange, one-touch, 522

Tool elimination
　as internal changeover improvement, 519–520
　by transferring tool functions, 316
Tool preparation errors, 560, 587, 615
Tools
　5-point check for orderliness, 256
　applying orderliness to, 307
　close storage site, 311
　color-coded orderliness, 308–309
　combining, 314, 315
　easy-to-maintain orderliness for, 307
　eliminating through orderliness, 313–316
　indicators, 308, 309
　machine-specific, 311
　outlined orderliness, 309
Tools placement, 222
　order of use, 222
Top-down improvements, 134–139
Torque tightening errors, 599
Torso motion, minimizing, 221
Total quality control (TQC), 36, 132
Total value added, 715
Training
　for basic safety, 698–699
　for multi-process operations, 407–413
　for multiple skills, 400
　in CCO, 708
　in Japanese *vs.* Western factories, 395
Training costs, for multi-process operations, 394–395
Transfer, 56, 57, 58
Transfer machine blade replacement, 528
Transparency, in multi-process operations, 405
Transparent operations, and standard operations, 628
Transport *kanban,* 443
Transport routes, 380–382
Transportation lead-time, 99
Two-handed task improvements, 644–645
　and safety, 704
Two-process flow production lines, 360

U

U-shaped manufacturing cells, 340, 360–362
　as condition for flow production, 341
　for multi-process operations, 395–396

Unbalanced capacity, 322
Unbalanced inventory, 161, 322
Union leadership, 84
Unmanned processes, 668
Unneeded equipment list, 767
Unneeded inventory list, 765, 766
Unneeded items
    moving out, 266
    separating from needed items, 266
    throwing out, 266
    types and disposal treatments, 277
    unneeded equipment list, 278
    unneeded inventory items list, 277
Unprocessed workpieces, set-up, 663, 668
Unprofitable factories, anatomy of, 38
Usability testing, and defect prevention,
    549–550
Use points, maximum proximity, 222
Usefulness, and value-added, 147

V

Value analysis (VA), 157
Value engineering (VE), 157
Value-added work, 85, 166
    JIT Management Diagnostic List, 717
    vs. wasteful motion, 86, 147
VCR assembly line, cooperative operations
    example, 429
Vertical development, 20, 24–27, 26, 378, 391
Vertical improvement makers, 167
Vibration switches, 574
    applications, 583
Visible 5Ss, 249–251, 252
    visible cleanliness, 253
    visible discipline, 254–255
    visible orderliness, 252–253
    visible proper arrangement, 251–252
    visibly cleaned up, 253
Visible cleanliness, 253
Visible discipline, 254–255
Visible orderliness, 252–253
    with signboard strategy, 295
Visible proper arrangement, 251–252
Visibly cleaned up, 253
Visual control, 26, 120, 231, 251, 723
    and *kaizen,* 471–473
    andon for, 456, 464–470

    as non-guarantee of improvements,
        453–454, 472–473
    defect prevention with, 563
    defective item displays for, 456, 457, 458
    error prevention through, 456, 458
    for safety, 700
    in JIT production, 10–11
    in *kanban* systems, 437
    kaizen boards for, 462
    kanban for, 456, 457
    management flexibility through, 419
    preventing communication errors with,
        556
    process display standing signboards,
        462–463
    production management boards for, 456,
        457, 470–471
    red demarcators, 455, 456
    red tag strategy for, 268–269, 455, 456
    signboard strategy, 455, 456
    standard operation charts for, 456, 457
    standing signboards for, 462–463
    through *kanban,* 440
    types of, 455–459
    visual orderliness case study, 459–462
    waste prevention with, 230–232
    white demarcators, 455, 456
Visual control tools, roles in improvement
    cycle, 473
Visual orderliness
    case study, 459–462
    in electronics parts storage area, 460
    signboard strategy for, 293–306
Visual proper arrangement, 17
Visual safety assurance, 707–708
Vocal pull production, 371, 372
Volume of orders, and production output, 61

W

Walking time, 635
Walking waste, 153–154, 173, 536
    eliminating for standard operations,
        645–649
Wall of fixed ideas, 210
Warehouse inventories, 161, 175
    as factory graveyards, 73
    reduction to zero, 20
Warehouse maintenance costs, 73

Warehouse waste, 69
Warning *andon,* 466–468
Warning devices, 567
Warning signals, 567
Washing unit, 364
    compact, 356
    in-line layout, 365
Waste, xii, 15, 643
    5MQS waste, 152–159
    and corresponding responses, 180
    and inventory, 48
    and motion, 75
    and red tag strategy, 269
    as everything but work, 182, 184, 191
    avoiding creation of, 226–236
    concealment by shish-kabob production,
        17, 158
    conveyance due to inventory, 90
    deeply embedded, 18, 150, 151
    defined, 146–150
    developing intuition for, 198
    eliminating with 5Ss, 508–511
    elimination by *kanban,* 440
    elimination through JIT production, xi, 8,
        341–342
    embedding and hiding, 84
    examples of motion as, 76
    hidden, 179
    hiding in conveyor flows, 67
    how to discover, 179–181, 179–198
    how to remove, 198–226
    identifying in changeover procedures,
        508–511
    in changeover procedures, 501
    in external changeover operations,
        510–511
    in internal changeover operations, 509–510
    in screw-fastening operation, 148
    inherited *vs.* inherent, 79–84
    invisible, 111
    JIT and cost reduction approach to, 69–71
    JIT Production System perspective, 152
    JIT seven types of, 172–179
    JITs seven types of, 172–179
    latent, 198
    making visible, 147
    minimizing through *kanban* systems, 437
    production factor waste, 159–172
    reasons behind, 146–150
    reinforcing by equipment improvements,
        111–112

    related to single large cleaning chamber,
        155
    removing, 84–86, 198–226
    severity levels, 171–172
    through computerization, 83
    total elimination of, 145, 152
    types of, 151–179
Waste checklists, 194–198
    five levels of magnitude, 195
    how to use, 195
    negative/positive statements, 197
    process-specific, 195, 196, 197, 198
    three magnitude levels, 197
    workshop-specific, 195
Waste concealment, 454
    by inventory, 326, 327
    revealing with one-piece flow, 350–351, 352
Waste discovery, 179–181
    back-door approach to, 181–183
    through current conditions analysis,
        185–198
    with arrow diagrams, 186–190
    with one-piece flow under current
        conditions, 183–185
    with operations analysis tables, 190–192
    with standard operations, 193–194
    with waste-finding checklists, 194–198
Waste prevention, 226, 228
    and do it now attitude, 236
    by avoiding fixed thinking, 235–236
    by outlining technique, 231
    by thorough standardization, 228–230
    with 5W1H sheet, 232–236
    with *andon,* 232
    with *kanban* system, 232
    with one-piece flow, 353
    with pitch and inspection buzzers, 232
    with red tagging, 231
    with signboards, 231
    with visual and auditory control, 230–232
Waste proliferation, 198, 199
Waste removal, 198–199
    50% implementation rate, 205–206
    and Basic Spirit principles for
        improvement, 204
    and denial of status quo, 205
    and eliminating fixed ideas, 204
    basic attitude for, 199–211
    by correcting mistakes, 207
    by cutting spending on improvements, 207
    by experiential wisdom, 210–211
    by Five Whys approach, 208–210

by using the brain, 208
in wasteful movement, 211–217
lot waiting waste, 219
positive attitude towards, 204–205
process waiting waste, 218
through combination charts for standard
operations, 223–226
wasteful human movement, 217–223
Waste transformation, 198
Waste-finding checklists, 737–743
process-specific, 739, 741, 742, 743
workshop-specific, 738, 740
Waste-free production, 49
Waste-related forms, 730
5W1H checklists, 744–746
arrow diagrams, 730–732
general flow analysis charts, 733–734
operations analysis charts, 735–736
waste-finding checklists, 737–743
Wasteful movement
and eliminating retention waste, 213–217
by people, 217–223
eliminating, 211, 213
Wastology, 145
Watch stem processes, 397, 398
Watching waste, 154
Weekly JIT improvement report, 846–848
Whirligig beetle *(mizusumashi)*, 465
Wire harness molding process, internal
changeover improvement case
study, 517–518
Withdrawal *kanban*, 444
Wood products factory, multi-process
operations in, 425
Work
as value-added functions, 182
meaning of, 74–75
motion and, 74–79
vs. motion, 657, 659
Work environment, comfort of, 223
Work methods chart, 627, 629, 829–830
Work operations, primacy over equipment
improvements, 103–108
Work sequence, 636
and standard operations, 625
arranging equipment according to, 638
for standard operations charts, 636
Work tables, ergonomics, 222
Work-in-process, 8
management, 81, 83
Work-to-motion ratio, 86
Work/material accumulation waste, 173

Worker hour minimization, 62, 66–69
Worker mobility, 19
Worker variations, 367–371
Workerless automation, 106
Workpiece directional errors, 605
Workpiece extraction, 663
Workpiece feeding, applying automation to,
665
Workpiece motion, waste in, 158–159
Workpiece pile-ups, 25, 118
Workpiece positioning errors, 605
Workpiece processing, applying *jidoka* to,
664
Workpiece removal
applying human automation to, 668
motor-driven chain for, 695
with processed cylinders, 667
Wrong part errors, 587, 612, 613
Wrong workpiece, 560, 587, 614

Y

Yen appreciation, xi

Z

Zero accidents, 699
Zero breakdowns, 684, 685
production maintenance cycle for, 687
with 5S approach, 241
Zero changeovers, with 5S approach, 242
Zero complaints, with 5S approach, 242
Zero defects, 545
5S strategy for, 565
human errors and, 562–563
information strategies, 563
machine cause strategies, 564
material cause strategies, 564
overall plan for achieving, 561–565
production maintenance cycle for, 687
production method causes and strategies,
564–565
with 5S approach, 241
Zero defects checklists
three-point evaluation, 619–620

three-point response, 620–622
using, 616–622
Zero delays, with 5S approach, 242
Zero injuries
strategies for, 699–709

with 5S approach, 241
Zero inventory, 20, 98–102
importance of faith in, 176
Zero red ink, with 5S approach, 242
Zigzag motions, avoiding, 221

About the Author

Hiroyuki Hirano believes Just-In-Time (JIT) is a theory and technique to thoroughly eliminate waste. He also calls the manufacturing process the equivalent of making music. In Japan, South Korea, and Europe, Mr. Hirano has led the on-site rationalization improvement movement using JIT production methods. The companies Mr. Hirano has worked with include:

Polar Synthetic Chemical Kogyo Corporation
Matsushita Denko Corporation
Sunwave Kogyo Corporation
Olympic Corporation
Ube Kyosan Corporation
Fujitsu Corporation
Yasuda Kogyo Corporation
Sharp Corporation and associated industries
Nihon Denki Corporation and associated industries
Kimura Denki Manufacturing Corporation and associated industries
Fukuda ME Kogyo Corporation
Akazashina Manufacturing Corporation
Runeau Public Corporation (France)
Kumho (South Korea)
Samsung Electronics (South Korea)
Samsung Watch (South Korea)
Sani Electric (South Korea)

Mr. Hirano was born in Tokyo, Japan, in 1946. After graduating from Senshu University's School of Economics, Mr. Hirano worked with Japan's largest computer manufacturer in laying the conceptual groundwork for the country's first full-fledged production management system. Using his own interpretation of the JIT philosophy, which emphasizes "ideas and techniques for the complete elimination of waste," Mr. Hirano went on to help bring the JIT Production Revolution to dozens of companies, including Japanese companies as well as major firms abroad, such as a French automobile manufacturer and a Korean consumer electronics company.

The author's many publications in Japanese include: *Seeing Is Understanding: Just-In-Time Production (Me de mite wakaru jasuto in taimu seisanh hoshiki)*, *Encyclopedia of Factory Rationalization (Kojo o gorika suru jiten)*, *5S Comics (Manga 5S)*, *Graffiti Guide to the JIT Factory Revolution (Gurafiti JIT kojo kakumei)*, and a six-part video tape series entitled *JIT Production Revolution, Stages I and II*. All of these titles are available in Japanese from the publisher, Nikkan Kogyo Shimbun, Ltd. (Tokyo).

In 1989, Productivity Press made Mr. Hirano's *JIT Factory Revolution: A Pictorial Guide to Factory Design of the Future* available in English.